'This is an excellent resource, providing counselling
tioners with a comprehensive guide to working safel
creatively with clients over the phone. I can't recom   ....gly
enough to existing phone therapists and to those who are considering working in
this way'.

– **Caroline Jesper**, *BACP Head of Professional Standards*

'Sarah's book is an accessible and detailed read, suitable for both experienced
therapists and trainees. I particularly like the way she interviewed therapists from
different theoretical orientations. As hybrid ways of working are now a part of
many therapists' working life, this book feels like an essential read for all'.

– **Rachel Golding**, *MBACP Senior Accred. Programme*
Tutor at The Counselling Foundation

Phone Therapy

Phone therapy is as relevant as it was 50 years ago. The increased use of this medium during the COVID-19 pandemic, and the revision of professional therapy body guidance, has endorsed the validity and effectiveness of phone therapy.

The book updates, revises and reinvigorates the medium for individual therapists, counselling services and training organisations in a post-lockdown world, where blended therapy is the norm. It includes practical considerations, phone-related theory, personal experience and self-reflection exercises. Contributing counsellor vignettes cover topics such as adapting theoretical modalities and EDI considerations without visual cues. From assessments, contracting and core skills to assumptions, disinhibition and privacy issues, it supports therapists and counselling organisations to embrace the accessibility, flexibility and creativity that therapy by phone provides.

Relevant for experienced and trainee therapists alike, this book provides practitioners with the support and knowledge to confidently use phone therapy in their practice.

Sarah Hart is a BACP-accredited therapist and supervisor, providing phone therapy supervision to therapists working for phone-delivered therapy services. She works in private practice for a charity and provides group supervision in a face-to-face setting. She has provided phone therapy for 14 years and phone therapy training for 11 years.

Phone Therapy

A Guide for Practitioners Working with Voice Alone

Sarah Hart

Routledge
Taylor & Francis Group

LONDON AND NEW YORK

Cover image: © Getty Images

First published 2023
by Routledge
4 Park Square, Milton Park, Abingdon, Oxon OX14 4RN

and by Routledge
605 Third Avenue, New York, NY 10158

Routledge is an imprint of the Taylor & Francis Group, an informa business

British Library Cataloguing-in-Publication Data
A catalogue record for this book is available from the British Library

Library of Congress Cataloging-in-Publication Data
A catalog record has been requested for this book

ISBN: 978-1-032-18201-8 (hbk)
ISBN: 978-1-032-18199-8 (pbk)
ISBN: 978-1-003-25339-6 (ebk)

DOI: 10.4324/9781003253396

Typeset in Times New Roman
by Apex CoVantage, LLC

MIX
Paper | Supporting responsible forestry
FSC
www.fsc.org   FSC™ C013985

Printed in the United Kingdom
by Henry Ling Limited

This book is dedicated to my husband Simon Richards, who listens deeply.

Listen thrice, think twice, speak once.

–Anonymous

Contents

Preface   xii
Acknowledgements   xv

1   **You can trust what you hear**   1

Hearing is our fastest sense 2
What is hearing exactly? 2
So how do we hear? 3
The pathway of sound 3
Frequency, amplitude and the soundtrack of Jaws *4*
Sudden noise and misophonia 4
Silence and heightened arousal 5
Hearing is always switched on 5
Theories of selective attention 6
The Cocktail Party Effect 6
'Halfalogues' 7
Hebbrian plasticity 7
How we manage degraded sound 7
Human sound, emotion and the therapeutic relationship 8

2   **Phone therapy uncovered**   10

The setting 10
How helplines differ from phone therapy 11
Limitations and benefits of phone therapy 12
Phone therapy's greatest attributes 13
Main differences between phone and face-to-face therapy 17

3   **Communication and core phone therapy skills**   20

Non-verbal communication and paralanguage 20
The therapist's voice 23
The effective therapeutic phone alliance 24

4   Theoretical modalities used in phone therapy   40

Person-centred 40
Psychodynamic 43
Integrative transpersonal 45
Pluralistic 48
Cognitive behavioural therapy 50

**5   The contract – working legally, professionally and ethically
on the phone**   53

Security and confidentiality relating to phones 53
Therapist's digital footprint 55
When and how to contract 57
Contracting with clients 58
Phone therapy contract with clients 59
The first session 65

6   Assessment, psychological suitability and risk   72

The phone therapy assessment 72
Assessing risk 76
*Working with eating disorders and substance abuse on the
    phone 82*
Referral and signposting pathways 86

7   Equality, diversity and inclusion within phone therapy   90

Disability 91
Hearing loss 95
Race and culture 98
Gender, sexual and relationship diversity (GSRD) 103
Older people 106
Children and young people 108

8   Creative interventions for phone therapy   115

Suggestions for safe creative working on the phone 120
Expressive writing therapy 121
Visualisation 122
Grounding the client during phone therapy 123

9   Considerations for supervision by phone   126

Phone supervision or supervision on the phone? 126
Models of online supervision 126
Adapting face-to-face supervision for the phone 127

Contracting and practicalities for supervision by phone 131

Helping the supervisee develop communication skills for phone therapy 132

Equality, diversity and inclusion (EDI) as part of phone supervision 133

Psychological suitability and managing risk during supervision 134

Understanding the context and legal implications of the supervisee's work 135

Choosing a phone therapy supervisor 136

Index   138

Preface

Therapy by phone has a 50-year history, and bolstered by research, it is a proven, valid therapy medium. As a therapist who has provided phone therapy for 14 years, delivered phone therapy training for 11 years and supervised phone therapy practice for nine years, I have known, since 2008, how effective, accessible and powerful the medium can be.

It was my experience, however, that other therapists tended to have a black and white opinion of phone therapy. Some, typically those who were attracted to my training courses or supervisees working for phone-delivered services, were as drawn to it as I am, valuing the intimacy of voice and hearing and the therapeutic asset of visual anonymity. Others felt anxious about working without being able to see their clients and some were simply not convinced that working therapeutically without being physically present with a client was really possible or ethical by any remote means.

Then, in early 2020, this viewpoint was challenged dramatically when the usual way we went about our lives and therapeutic practice changed almost overnight. The COVID-19 pandemic spread like wildfire, and lockdowns, curfews and quarantines around the world forced many therapists who were inexperienced or sceptical of phone and online therapy to make a hasty decision – start working with clients via digital media or face a sudden rupture of unknown duration to the therapeutic alliance. The therapy community was in crisis.

The result was that therapist apprehension and ambivalence gave way to a growing acceptance that therapy can take place in media rather than face to face. The practice of both phone therapy and online therapy burgeoned overnight. Half of my clients, those in my private practice who were already having phone therapy, remained unaffected by the sudden change, and I hastily transitioned my face-to-face clients from my work within a counselling organisation to the phone. As a phone therapy trainer, I was overwhelmed by demand for my services from therapy services, therapy training organisations and individual practitioners wanting to develop their skills to work professionally and proficiently on the phone.

By mid-2020, I was approached by my professional body, the British Association for Counselling and Psychotherapy (BACP) to form part of a hastily convened Expert Reference Group (ERG) to review and revise the BACP's 2016

Telephone and E-counselling competences. The ERG consisted of experts in the field of digital therapy including representatives from the BACP, academic institutions, online training providers and core practitioner training courses. In early 2021, the BACP-revised guidance, renamed Online and Phone Therapy (OPT) competence framework, was published. OPT – online and phone therapy – is the term I use throughout this book to refer to remote or digital therapy that occurs when the therapist and the client are not physically present.

The wider therapy community within the UK and globally now recognises that the landscape of therapy has changed. Whether or not it was welcomed or adequately prepared for, digital therapy became mainstream. The BACP now regards online and phone therapy as a setting for therapy as opposed to a specialism provided by a minority of practitioners with a particular interest and experience in text (mainly synchronous and asynchronous emails), video and phone therapy. As a result of the pandemic, trainee therapists were for the first time permitted to work on the phone and online with clients as part of their BACP training placements. BACP accredited therapist training, and no doubt most courses accredited by other professional bodies will now include OPT training modules as part of their core curriculum. Many experienced therapists and therapy services have discovered the unexpected advantages regarding the work of therapy at a distance and among other benefits are embracing the opportunity of accessibility and flexibility for clients and therapists alike. Therapy services and individual practitioners and clients have welcomed the option of a choice of face-to-face, phone or online or blended therapy (using a combination of these) beyond COVID-19 lockdown.

It is clear that in spite of technological advances and the growing interest in online therapy, therapy by phone is still a popular choice. It is endorsed by the BACP, which clearly recognises it of equal value to online as it offers something different. In addition to the simplicity of the medium for client and therapist, therapy by phone provides something very intimate – voice alone, directly into the ear, which can be used very powerfully to convey meaning and understanding – there is something primal about this. Phone therapists need to listen very carefully and in my experience, the ability to listen increases with practice, which is borne out by research on information processing by Broadbent (1958).

The purpose of this book is to share my experience of working therapeutically without visual cues from the client. I have drawn on training material I have developed over more than a decade, the new revisions decided by the BACP and the contributions of other professional bodies and therapists who work on the phone to champion phone therapy's validity and efficacy.

Although the phone has been in existence for nearly 150 years, the book aims to update its application in the therapeutic world as well as considering its use in the exciting future of working in the twenty-first century at a distance, beyond the COVID-19 pandemic. At the end of my teleconference-delivered training course, some therapists go as far as saying that working via the phone has rejuvenated their practice and that they are as passionate as I am about therapy via phone. Whether you are an experienced practitioner or a trainee therapist, my sincere hope is that this book will increase your knowledge, help develop your competence and boost your confidence for phone therapy. If you join the ranks of therapists who are passionate about working on the phone, so much the better!

Reference

Broadbent, D. E. (1958). *Perception and communication* (Reprint ed.). Pergamon Press.

Acknowledgements

Thank you to all therapists who enjoy working on the phone, who champion the medium, many of whom I have trained and some being my supervisees. Your opinions and feedback encouraged me to write this book.

I owe special thanks to all the therapists who contributed their knowledge and experience within various chapters. Without the generous sharing of your expertise and time, the book would have been considerably less informative and varied.

I appreciate the support of my supervisors Rachel Golding and Rosie Lyden, who have been sounding boards on a number of topics. To my colleagues at Tilehouse Counselling, thanks to Sue Barnes for her confidence and the team for their writing progress enquiries.

Thank you to my patient, reassuring friends and family, particularly my children Roxane and Brett for their belief in me. To Simon for listening and his steadfast love.

I also thank the staff members at Routledge who have been involved in producing and promoting this book.

Chapter 1

You can trust what you hear

Having delivered phone therapy training for over a decade, I have heard sceptical opinions and been asked anxious questions about whether therapy via phone is effective, safe or even possible without seeing a client. In his book *Using Counselling Skills on the Telephone*, Sanders (2007, p. 23) refers to what he calls an 'intellectual inertia' regarding whether counselling can be done when working face to face. He believes that therapists made assumptions based on received wisdom about what was and was not possible.

In a systematic review of comparative studies by Irvine et al. (2020) which focused on the interactional differences between psychotherapeutic encounters conducted face to face versus by phone, Antonioni (1973) was cited as noting that 'despite empirical studies consistently showing no significant difference in interactional features of alliance, empathy and so on, therapists remain ambivalent about the use of the medium'. He suggests that 'this contradiction stems from counsellors believing that they rely more on visual than auditory cues, and hence perceiving an inferiority of the telephone medium – despite objective clinical evidence not supporting this viewpoint'.

I agree that this used to be the case, particularly before the global COVID-19 pandemic, when experienced practitioners and trainee therapists alike were forced to consider digital media or abruptly end therapy with clients. Before COVID-19, BACP-accredited core therapy training didn't include online or phone therapy elements, but now that the BACP regards digital therapy as a setting for therapeutic communication rather than a specialism, this view has changed.

Having provided phone therapy to clients since 2008, I know it works. I learnt that I can trust the medium and if and when risk occurs, I have procedures in place to manage this. What this means is that I have learnt to trust my ears. Trusting my hearing doesn't mean that I don't trust the therapeutic value of sight in the therapy room or on video. It means that when I work without seeing my client, I know that my sense of hearing and the ability to process what I hear can and does give me the information I need to do the work of a therapist.

I hope this chapter will allow you to regard your auditory sense with an increased interest and greater understanding. Through the lens of neuroscience and cognitive science, let's consider our most vital piece of equipment, the greatest resource for phone therapy – our ears.

DOI: 10.4324/9781003253396-1

Hearing is our fastest sense

It's our auditory system not our visual that reacts first and provides information for us to work out how to respond. Hearing tends to be better at separating inputs properly even though it gathers information from a much wider region, which isn't limited by line of sight. This is why hearing is faster than vision. An auditory stimulus only takes 8–10 milliseconds to reach the brain (Kemp, 1973) while a visual stimulus takes 20–40 milliseconds (Marshall, 1943). By contrast, reaction time to touch is intermediate, at 155 milliseconds (Robinson, 1934). On an evolutionary level, our auditory system is our first sense to start to process whether something is familiar and safe or a threat which we must counter in some way.

In his book *The Universal Sense*, auditory neurologist Horowitz (2012, p. 111) writes,

> You can be startled by sound, touch, or balance but not by vision, taste or smell. This is because these first three sensory systems are mechanosensory systems, relying on rapid mechanical opening of neurotransmitter channels that fire a very fast, evolutionarily very old neuronal circuit to activate spinal motor neurons and arousal circuits in your brain.

Just to be clear, being startled isn't necessarily about being frightened, it's an evolutionary response. It increases our arousal both physiologically, our senses, and psychologically, our emotional responses.

Horowitz (2012, p. 113) notes the contentious differences of opinion in trying to identify the neurobiological underpinnings of emotions. 'But one thing that is consistent in studies of emotion using techniques ranging from nineteenth-century psychology through twenty-first-century neural imaging is that one of the most important and fastest-acting triggers for emotion is sound, distributed throughout the cerebral cortex'.

That sound is the fastest trigger for emotion doesn't surprise me. Miller (1973) noted that on the phone, the speaker's lips are only inches away from the listener's ear, creating an unusual type of intimacy. My experience of phone therapy is that there is something primal about it, someone speaking directly into your ear creating a profound intimacy. A closeness of observation which, when coupled with how we are able to use our voices to convey understanding and empathy, creates a powerful therapeutic environment which we will explore in detail in Chapter 3.

As phone therapy occurs using one sense alone, having a closer look at how our hearing works can help us understand and learn to trust our amazing ability to hear.

What is hearing exactly?

We might think that in being present and mindful, we are actually hearing, seeing, touching, smelling the world around us but aren't. We are in fact interpreting a representation of the world by remapping the initial energy of any sensory stimulus which we initially experience as a sensation. After a stimulus comes perception, the integration of sensations which is the way we construct and experience the world around us. Therefore, hearing is the ability to perceive sounds by detecting vibrations and place meaning to that sound. In other words, we don't hear music, voices, traffic or client's voice – we notice vibrations.

So how do we hear?

It's complex and there are a lot of highly scientific books and research that explain this in detail; so, this is a brief explanation. Our auditory system is divided into two parts, the 'peripheral' and the 'central'. The peripheral system consists of three parts.

> *The outer ear* which is made up of the pinna (or auricle), the largely cartilaginous projecting portion of the external ear, as well as the ear canal and the eardrum.
>
> *The middle ear* is a narrow, air-filled space housing three tiny bones called the malleus, incus and stapes, collectively known as the ossicles. The eardrum in the outer ear is connected to malleus and the stapes, which is the smallest bone in the body, which is connected to the inner ear.
>
> *The inner ear* has two jobs. It changes electrical signals or nerve impulses into sound waves, and it is responsible for balance. The coiled hearing part of the inner ear is called the cochlea which comes from the Greek word for snail. The fluid-filled cochlea contains four rows of many thousands of tiny sensory cells or hair cells.

The cochlea is connected to the second part of our auditory system, the central hearing system, which through the pathway explained in the following, is the journey from the auditory nerve to the brain.

The pathway of sound

The outer ear channels sound waves into the ear canal from the outside world. This is not necessarily as simple as it sounds as sound waves can be refracted, reflected, distorted and absorbed, losing strength and cohesion depending on how many things get in the way.

Sound waves travel down the ear canal to the eardrum, which vibrates the three little bones of the inner ear, the malleus, incus and stapes. This movement leads to pressure waves which make the fluid inside the cochlea move. The fluid movement in the inner ear makes the tiny hairs in the cochlea bend and wave. Amazingly, the hair cells are tuned to respond to different pitch or frequency of sounds. High-pitch sound waves stimulate the hairs in the lower part of the cochlea and low-pitched sound waves move the hairs in the upper part. Each hair cell detects the pitch or frequency of sound waves to which it is tuned to respond and then converts the sound waves into electrical signals.

The electrical signals are sent via an extraordinarily complex pathway through the brain stem to the auditory cortex, the hearing centre of the brain which converts them to meaningful sound.

Frequency, amplitude and the soundtrack of *Jaws*

Frequency is the number of times per second that a sound pressure wave repeats itself. Units of frequency are called hertz (Hz), which means cycles per second. Frequencies above 20,000 Hz are known as ultrasound and very low-frequency sounds at the opposite end of the spectrum (below 20 Hz) are known as infrasound. There is plenty of fascinating research about animals being able to use ultrasound, dogs for example, and infrasound, such as elephants, dolphins, mice and snakes. Humans with normal hearing can hear sounds between 20 Hz and 20,000 Hz, but most speech frequencies are in the 100 Hz to 4000 Hz range.

Frequency measures the cycle rate of a sound wave and pitch is how high or low it sounds when you hear it. Having longer vocal cords, male voices are typically at the lower frequency of around 100–200 Hz; female voices fall into the range of about 120–350 Hz, and a child's range is 250–400 Hz. Pitch is the perception of how high or low a sound seems. The higher the frequency the higher the pitch of the sound you hear. You will find more on pitch in Chapter 3 when we consider how people use their voices and what this might mean when we work without seeing our clients.

Amplitude is the strength of sound waves that we perceive as volume or loudness. Decibel (dB) is named after Alexander Graham Bell, who invented the telephone in 1847. As engineers needed to measure the audio levels in telephone circuits, the sound measurement unit known as bel was coined in honour of Bell. A decibel is one-tenth of a bel, and the decibel scale is still used to monitor sound that could harm our hearing. A normal conversation registers around 60 dB, the volume of a whisper is about 30 db.

A low frequency, high in decibels, will mean a loud, low pitch and when this occurs, it triggers an evolved fear response within us. Loud and low means a large predator is nearby. Think of the hair-raising response we have when we hear the guttural, low roar of a lion which is about 25 times as loud as a petrol lawnmower (Klemuk et al., 2011). One of the most iconic film scores, John Williams's soundtrack for *Jaws* is played by a tuba. The tuba is a very low-pitched instrument and perceptually, Williams's 'Da-dum. Da-dum. Da-dum' was created to strike fear as we are hardwired to perceive that the lower the frequency, the larger the threat (Horowitz, 2012).

Sudden noise and misophonia

Fortunately, loud, low pitches are unlikely to commonly occur in a phone therapy setting, but it's worth noting that sudden noises can still startle us as we might react to these like a response to a false alarm. An unexpected noise can leave us feeling irritated or angry, something we might like to be aware of considering the potential for therapist disinhibition when not physically present with a client. Working with only one sense, a sudden noise of some sort might trigger a surprised response from a therapist. Being startled isn't the only trigger. Misophonia, also known as Selective Sound Sensitivity, is the strong emotional response to the presence or anticipation of a sound. People with misophonia experience three key emotional responses: anger, disgust and anxiety, with anger being the predominant emotion, accompanied by high levels of arousal, the fight-or-flight response. Notably, trigger sounds are often human and include sounds such as loud breathing, swallowing, chewing and sniffing. Other triggers are keyboard or finger tapping or sounds associated with movement like fidgeting (Brout et al., 2018). Being aware of our potential for what might seem a puzzling emotional response to sound made by our clients could be useful for avoiding knee-jerk responses due to disinhibition when working on the phone.

Silence and heightened arousal

Without knowing how to handle a silence during phone therapy, it can feel anxiety provoking when a client stops talking. This is because a lack of sound increases our attention and arousal, increasing our ear's sensitivity. It seems that silence heightens our emotional vigilance. Neurobiologists Denis Paré and Dawn Collins (2000) found that a period of silence after a series of tones used in an experiment showed an increase in conditioned responses was linked to learning about unpleasant or frightening stimuli.

It's not that a sudden silence is fear-provoking in itself, but it warns the brain that something is amiss, alerting us that something potentially bad is about to happen. Knowing that silence causes arousal, we can better understand how it's possible to feel more uncomfortable with client silences when we work on the phone compared to working face to face. Managing silence whether this is about a process or a technical difficulty will be explored in other chapters.

Hearing is always switched on

Unlike our visual system, our auditory system is continuously switched 'on', so we always hear things. As the scope of our hearing is wider than sound, it stimulates some of our most important subconscious and conscious processes.

Although we aren't consciously aware of it, our auditory system is continually monitoring background noise for any change that is significant and might require our attention. It is the only sense that still operates when we're sleeping. Even when we sleep, the Riticular Activating System, the bundle of nerves that connect that subconscious part of our brain with the conscious part of our brain is always listening, evaluating whether it should wake us up to take care of something that is important.

Theories of selective attention

When we're awake we don't pay attention to every passing sound, we would be overwhelmed if we did. Instead, we have the ability to focus on important information occurring around us. Selective attention is the process of focusing our awareness on a relevant stimulus while ignoring irrelevant stimuli around us (Goldstein, 2001). It allows us to limit how much information we process at any one time.

Experimental psychologist Donald Broadbent (1958) was one of the first theorists of selective attention. Broadbent's theory of attention was known as a filter or bottleneck model. He proposed that we can't consciously process all sensory information around us at any one time; so, information is bottlenecked, allowing us to filter information to avoid overload. To test his theory, Broadbent used what is known as the dichotic listening task, simultaneously sending one message to a person's right ear and a different message to their left ear. Through this experiment, he found that instead of repeating back the message in the order they were presented, people tended to repeat back what was heard in one ear followed by the other ear and made fewer mistakes when they did so. Broadbent's observations led him to conclude, 'The nervous system acts like a single communication channel where the inputs to one sense dominate those being received through other senses'. What this means is our hearing is heightened when we can't see or hear or touch. Although later theories take how our attention can shift into account, the intensity of therapy without sight, can in my experience, feel like our hearing dominates other senses and takes the lead as we tune into what the client presents. I think this is why intimacy and closeness are often used to describe phone therapy.

Other theorists such as Anne Treisman (1960), one of Broadbent's students who specialised in cognitive psychology, took a wider approach to selective attention. Treisman proposed that we have an early selection filter which allows important information, like hearing someone call our name, to seep through when our attention is elsewhere, which leads us to Colin Cherry's listening experiments.

The Cocktail Party Effect

The Cocktail Party Effect (Cherry, 1953) is the remarkable ability we have to tune in to one person talking when we are in a busy, noisy environment like a cocktail party. Even in a crowded room, we are able to focus on what we need or want to hear relatively easily by muting out other voices and sounds. We are able to group together cues we hear, changes in amplitude across their different frequencies, and our brains interpret these as coming from the same sound source. Also, we pick up on fluctuations in sound in a noisy room and our auditory system is able to fill in the gaps by grouping obscured words (McDermott, 2009).

It seems that other non-human animals have a Cocktail Party Effect experience when it comes to identifying mates, rivals or enemies at night with many other creatures vocalising at once. For example without visual cues, many frogs use conspecific vocalisations, sounds that only their species make to locate each other while hundreds of other frogs around them do the same (McDermott, 2009). Being able to zone in and focus fully is essential for being able to function in a world of sensory overload. It could be particularly useful if there is a background noise in the phone's client setting, a young person who has a music-playing device near their bedroom door so as not to be overheard, for instance.

'Halfalogues'

Interestingly, there is an annoying exception to our ability to filter out irrelevant sounds and this is when we overhear a 'halfalogue' – only one side of a phone conversation. Lauren Emberson (Emberson et al., 2010), a developmental cognitive neuroscientist, found that hearing only half a phone conversation distracts us because we can't predict the succession of speech. As we can't anticipate the conversation with any degree of certainty or close our ears, we are distracted and if the caller speaks loudly or uses words that cause alarm – 'police' or 'ambulance' for instance – it increases the stimulus.

What are the implications of phone therapy? This could be a privacy issue for clients – family members in the house or other people nearby might have their ears pricked unwittingly. The crucial matter of ensuring privacy as much as possible is covered in Chapter 5, but for now, because we know that halfalogues heighten everyone's hearing, unless either party has a hearing impairment (discussed in Chapter 7), the use of earphones is recommended.

Hebbrian plasticity

It also appears that we can quickly tune in to a sound that is memorable or recognisable to us. In a noisy environment you might notice your attention suddenly being diverted by a sound of interest like hearing your name, your partner's voice or an accent that is familiar to you. Familiarity of a specific voice or speech pattern will activate auditory neural patterns we have heard before. This form of neural learning is known as Hebbrian plasticity – on hearing something numerous times, we improve our efficiency of responding. This is the brain's ability to rewire itself to speed up responses to previously encountered events (Horowitz, 2012). In addition to building the therapeutic relationship on the phone, without sight, I wonder whether neural learning helps us to tune into our client's voice, perhaps without sight even heightening our hearing when we work on the phone.

How we manage degraded sound

Holdgraf et al. (2016) found that this neural plasticity of the brain facilitates the extraction of speech-like features even when listening to degraded input. They performed spectrotemporal receptive field (STRF) plasticity analysis on electrophysiological data from recordings obtained directly from the human audi-tory cortex. Simply put, they found that the brain emphasises word-like sounds, filters out competing noise and that these rapid-tuning abilities can be improved by experience. Maybe this explains why on occasions when the phone line is not completely clear or if a client has an accent, we are able to tune in and understand more than we might expect. It's not always possible of course, a poor line might mean a session is interrupted or that a client with an accent is referred, but it might help us to know that because of brain plasticity, our auditory process is more adept at tuning in to speech than perhaps we realise.

Human sound, emotion and the therapeutic relationship

Melanie Aeschlimann et al. (2008) studied emotional expression and hearing, focusing on non-linguistic human sounds such as laughter, cries, erotic sounds and non-human sounds including those of an alarm clock and typewriter. They found that sounds which had negative emotional responses were perceived as louder even when they were at the same amplitude as other sounds. Sounds that were rated highly by the respondents were those that were regarded as emotion-ally positive. But the sounds that evoke the greatest emotional response in us are those that are made by humans.

Although our attention is stimulated by many noises around us, sounds made by living creatures create an emotional response because they are harmonic. It's easier for us to hear human sounds, audible cues, in addition to speech, and they tend to stand out for us more if there is background noise. We are able to respond more quickly to sounds we have heard before and we are able to process low-level sensory information such as changes to tone and loudness faster than the complexity of speech.

Much is written elsewhere about how we hear, indeed about all of our senses and to learn more about this provides fascinating considerations for the therapy. From this chapter's brief explanation of how our auditory process occurs and brief exploration of neuroscience and cognitive science relating to hearing, we can be sure that as therapists, we can trust that our hearing can guide us to respond appropriately and with empathy to our clients when we work on the phone. More than this, we can use our voices verbally as well as without speech to convey very powerfully, our understanding and willingness to understand the client's world.

References

Aeschlimann, M., Knebel, J. F., Murray, M. M., & Clarke, S. (2008). Emotional pre-eminence of human vocalizations. *Brain Topography*, *20*(4), 239–248. https://doi.org/10.1007/s10548-008-0051-8

Broadbent, D. E. (1958). *Perception and communication* (Reprint ed.). Pergamon Press.

Brout, J. J., Edelstein, M., Erfanian, M., Mannino, M., Miller, L. J., Rouw, R., Kumar, S., & Rosenthal, M. Z. (2018). Investigating misophonia: A review of the empirical literature, clinical implications, and a research agenda. *Frontiers in Neuroscience, 12*. https://doi. org/10.3389/fnins.2018.00036

Cherry, E. C. (1953). Some experiments on the recognition of speech, with one and with two ears. *The Journal of the Acoustical Society of America, 25*(5), 975–979. https://doi. org/10.1121/1.1907229

Emberson, L. L., Lupyan, G., Goldstein, M. H., & Spivey, M. J. (2010). Overheard cell-phone conversations. *Psychological Science, 21*(10), 1383–1388. https://doi. org/10.1177/0956797610382126

Goldstein, B. E. (2001). *Sensation and perception* (6th ed.). Wadsworth Publishing.

Holdgraf, C. R., de Heer, W., Pasley, B., Rieger, J., Crone, N., Lin, J. J., Knight, R. T., & Theunissen, F. E. (2016). Rapid tuning shifts in human auditory cortex enhance speech intelligibility. *Nature Communications, 7*(1). https://doi.org/10.1038/ncomms13654

Horowitz, S. (2012). *The universal sense: How hearing shapes the mind*. Bloomsbury.

Irvine, A., Drew, P., Bower, P., Brooks, H., Gellatly, J., Armitage, C. J., Barkham, M., McMillan, D., & Bee, P. (2020). Are there interactional differences between telephone and face-to-face psychological therapy? A systematic review of comparative studies. *Journal of Affective Disorders, 265*, 120–131. https://doi.org/10.1016/j.jad.2020.01.057

Kemp, B. J. (1973). Reaction time of young and elderly subjects in relation to perceptual deprivation and signal-on versus signal-off conditions. *Developmental Psychology, 8*(2), 268–272. https://doi.org/10.1037/h0034147

Klemuk, S. A., Riede, T., Walsh, E. J., & Titze, I. R. (2011). Adapted to roar: Functional morphology of tiger and lion vocal folds. *PLoS One, 6*(11), e27029. https://doi. org/10.1371/journal.pone.0027029

Marshall, W. H., Talbot, S. A., & Ades, H. W. (1943). Cortical response of the anesthetized cat to gross photic and electrical afferent stimulation. *Journal of Neurophysiology, 6*(1), 1–15. https://doi.org/10.1152/jn.1943.6.1.1

McDermott, J. H. (2009). The cocktail party problem. *Current Biology, 19*(22), R1024–R1027. https://doi.org/10.1016/j.cub.2009.09.005

Miller, W. B. (1973). The telephone in outpatient psychotherapy. *American Journal of Psychotherapy, 27*(1), 15–26. https://doi.org/10.1176/appi.psychotherapy.1973.27.1.15

Paré, D., & Collins, D. R. (2000). Neuronal correlates of fear in the lateral amygdala: Multiple extracellular recordings in conscious cats. *The Journal of Neuroscience, 20*(7), 2701–2710. https://doi.org/10.1523/jneurosci.20-07-02701.2000

Robinson, S. H. (1934). Practical psychology in refractive work. *Clinical and Experimental Optometry, 17*(1), 17–22. https://doi.org/10.1111/j.1444-0938.1934.tb05905.x

Sanders, P. (2007). *Using counselling skills on the telephone* (3rd ed.). PCCS.

Treisman, A. M. (1960). Contextual cues in selective listening. *Quarterly Journal of Experimental Psychology, 12*(4), 242–248. https://doi.org/10.1080/17470216008416732

Chapter 2

Phone therapy uncovered

About ten years ago, I was asked to provide a definition of phone therapy to a judge. Having a niche private therapy practice working with parents, mainly mothers who live apart from their children, my clients are frequently trying to resolve child residency and contact orders through family courts. The judge in the case had ordered that my client received an insight-based therapy and when she told the court that this was taking place via phone, the validity of the medium was queried.

At that time, and indeed until fairly recently, online and phone therapy was considered a specialism. It was regarded as a specialist area of therapy offered by a minority of practitioners who understood and knew the value of working either on the phone or online via video or by synchronous and asynchronous email. As the majority of therapists chose to practice only when face to face with clients, questions about the efficacy of my practice were asked fairly regularly.

Phone therapy has been in existence for over 50 years. It is a tried-and-tested medium. In its simplest form, a session can take place between two landlines, not vastly different from the technology invented by Alexander Graham Bell. It's been almost 150 years since Bell carried out the first bidirectional telephone transmission of clear speech with his assistant. The technology we currently use to make calls on landlines will end in 2025, in the UK, and is being replaced with an internet-based version – the end of an era. For many people, the change will be as simple as plugging their home phone into their broadband router as landline calls will be delivered over digital technology called Voice over Internet Protocol (VoIP), which uses a Wi-Fi connection.

In addition to landlines, phone sessions take place between mobile phones – smart or basic – and online via a videoconferencing platform using audio only. None of these methods are necessarily any better than the other, the choice is determined largely by accessibility and quality of transmission. For example some clients might only have a basic mobile phone without internet capacity and others, like many people these days, might not have a landline.

The setting

Phone and online therapy is now widely regarded as the setting for therapeutic communication. It is acknowledged and accepted that therapy takes place when

DOI: 10.4324/9781003253396-2

the therapist and the client are not physically present via media that many of us now use in all other areas of our lives. The media used is constantly evolving and no doubt therapeutic practice will move with technological changes too.

My own definition for phone therapy is:

Phone therapy occurs when a therapist and client who are not physically together, use voice and hearing for therapeutic communication in the form of pre-arranged, contracted therapy sessions.

How helplines differ from phone therapy

Helplines, support lines, hotlines and listening services have a long history. In 1953, Chad Varah, a vicar in London, answered the first phone call from the Samaritans forming the suicide crisis line service delivered by 20,000 volunteers today. In the wake of the Samaritans, other helplines were established and nowadays, support lines exist for a wide range of issues. Support by phone line has not diminished since the emergence of online chatrooms and message boards, they sit alongside these internet services. To give some idea of scale, the UK-based Helplines Partnership, who provides a nationally recognised helpline standard, has a membership of over 350 helplines, and many other support lines exist in addition to this membership.

Support lines offer invaluable service to those who need to talk, who need advice, who are lonely, fearful, bullied, persecuted, discriminated against and worse, but this is not what is regarded as therapy via phone. Helplines typically offer immediate, one-off support by allowing the caller to express their current feelings and worries as well as ask questions. Sometimes, the call is answered immediately, particularly crisis lines. Other support agencies might phone the caller back after they have left a message. Helplines can be delivered by trained volunteers or paid staff, some of whom might be trained counsellors. In the UK, the Helplines Partnership has a recognised quality standard which defines and accredits best practice in helpline work.

The key difference between what helplines provide and therapy is that helpline staff use active listening skills to offer empathy, compassion without judgement and sometimes provide information and signposting, usually in a single call. Phone therapy is provided via contracted sessions, usually 50 minutes or one hour, booked in advance, often weekly on a short term or an ongoing basis. Depending on the therapist's modality and the client's needs, therapy facilitates the client to explore their feelings, thoughts and behaviour regarding their presenting issues, past and present relationships and life events with the intention of supporting the client to achieve change.

Provide clarity about what you offer

Attitudes are changing and particularly as a result of the COVID-19 pandemic, clients are likely to be more familiar with remote working for all manner of professional services than they have ever been. Even so, clarifying expectations are an important part of working ethically, particularly when you aren't physically present with a client.

A starting point is a description of what therapy is and how it can help clients. An explanation of how phone therapy works will reassure clients and manage any assumptions. For instance, as the medium for therapy is quite often the same as the initial enquiry, the client might think that you are on call and available for them to access during certain hours. Make sure that your online presence, your website and online listings include an explanation of how what you offer is different from a helpline, advice line or crisis line. That you will not be available 24 hours a day. Include information about what a client can do if they are in crisis and provide phone numbers for relevant agencies and crisis lines who can help. You might like to include your availability and give the client an idea of how quickly you will respond to enquiries, perhaps that you will endeavour to reply within 24 or 48 hours after receiving an email.

Clearly communicate the process of arranging therapy. Let the client know, for example, that after their enquiry, an initial 50-minute session will be arranged and your contract and maybe assessment questionnaires will be sent in advance. Another clear difference between helpline and therapy which is important to communicate is that either you or the counselling service you work for charges a fee for sessions, assuming that you do. Also, whether a limited number of contracted sessions will be available if you work to a short-term model. More details about initial contact with a client and arranging a session are included in Chapter 5.

Limitations and benefits of phone therapy

Limitations

The BACP Online and Phone Therapy (OPT) competence framework (2021) states that therapists need to discuss the potential limitations and benefits of phone and online therapy. To my mind, talking about therapy via the medium of the phone should be present not only at the initial stages but also throughout the work with the client as circumstances change. In addition to the limitations and benefits, I discuss the client's experience of therapy via the phone with them if they bring it up and also when I feel it is pertinent to do so during the work. Without visuals, we don't see or experience the therapy room in its physical sense, and we don't see each other. Talking about how we will work, how we are working, what comes up for and between us when there are no visual cues is all part of the collaboration which is phone therapy.

The BACP's list of *limitations* relevant to phone therapy included in the OPT competency framework: potential technical data security issues; a lack of visual contact in some approaches may reduce non-verbal communication which might impact on mutual understanding; that the remote nature of the work has the potential for exacerbating client circumstance (e.g. isolation).

I agree that we need to be aware of these potential limitations. I regard all of the above as matters that therapists and therapy services need to discuss with their clients and manage throughout the work with the client. More on how to do this is covered in subsequent chapters about privacy, risk, mental health and so on.

Benefits

BACP-listed examples of *benefits* of phone therapy include accessibility for clients with certain disabilities, those with limited transport options and clients living some distance away can receive therapy at home. Flexibility, that sessions can fit around client's life choices. Also, that being in separate locations may feel less inhibiting and the remote nature of the work has the potential for alleviating client circumstance, for example isolation.

Without a doubt, I have found the OPT competency framework's list to be beneficial to clients. You will find many more examples of my own and other practitioners peppered throughout this book. I hope these will help alleviate any doubt and anxiety about working with only audio.

Phone therapy's greatest attributes

When I train practitioners, I always refer to some of the phone therapy research spanning over the past five decades as I think it validates and helps build confidence for the medium. Feeling confident about phone therapy is a sound basis for affirming its efficacy when we talk to clients. Perhaps, one of the biggest limitations to phone therapy is practitioner anxiety, described by Brenes et al. (2012) as follows, 'Therapists may have a harder time adapting to telephone-delivered psychotherapy than clients, as they may be concerned about their ability to establish an effective therapeutic relationship in the absence of a face-to-face relationship'. I start validating phone therapy from the first contact with clients.

Accessibility and inhibition

A study by Reese et al. (2006) showed that telephone counselling clients reported that convenience, accessibility, control and inhibition were the most attractive attributes of receiving counselling (not crisis intervention) via the telephone. Of the 186 counselling clients who responded to the survey, 96% would be willing to seek telephone counselling again compared with 63.1% who reported being willing to seek face-to-face counselling. So, in this study, more than half (58%) of the respondents who had experienced both telephone and face-to-face counselling preferred telephone counselling.

This research shows that once clients try phone therapy, they quite frequently prefer it. Some of my clients talk regularly about differences and advantages and I encourage discussion about their experience. Certainly, convenience is regularly spoken about, no need to factor in travel time, find a parking space or walk from the train station or bus stop or pay for the cost of travel. Not having to go out on a dark winter's night is appreciated by us both.

Beyond convenience, there is considerable research highlighting how without the medium of the phone, therapy would not have taken place (Lynch et al. (1997), Swinson et al. (1995), de Leo et al. (2002)). Convenience of the medium became an almost overnight necessity when the threat posed by the COVID-19 pandemic required a hasty transition from face to face to the phone. I hope new research will be undertaken about this experience.

Reese et al.'s (2006) research shows that on the phone, clients are able to feel less inhibited. Uninhibited expression means that clients feel less constrained on the phone but still able to retain their sense of control of their responses. When not seen by the therapist, clients often feel better able to express themselves naturally and freely. By contrast, the psychological phenomenon of 'toxic disinhibition' (Suler, 2004) is what occurs when a client and indeed therapist, impulsively, without restraint expresses themselves beyond what is considered within the realms of social norms when not physically present. It is worth noting that Reese et al. consider disinhibition to be the opposite of inhibition, which is akin to what Suler calls 'benign disinhibtion'. Suler's online disinhibition effect will be explored in relation to working without seeing in the next chapter.

Attentiveness, focus, closeness and safety

Research by Reese et al. (2002) into free telephone counselling offered to the employees of three large Fortune 500 companies as well as other smaller, regional companies across the United States showed that telephone counselling appears to be an 'effective psychological practice and without an office, clothes and physical appearance to potentially distract them, clients being counselled via phone may be inclined to focus better on what the therapist says'.

Not being seen can allow clients to focus on themselves as well as listen more attentively to what the therapist says, but what about therapist attentiveness? Spizman (2001) developed a measure rating patient's experience of their therapist's listening behaviour. Patients were asked to rate how much they felt their therapist listened to them, how caring the therapist was and how much the patient liked their therapist. Interestingly, the therapists in this study believed that treatment via the phone would be less effective than face to face; however, the clients did not show a difference in belief regarding the phone's effectiveness. In fact, the clients reported a more significant relationship with the therapists when receiving treatment via the phone compared to those clients in the face-to-face setting.

Perhaps, client focus and being able to receive the therapist's attentiveness is due to a heightened sense of hearing – explored in the previous chapter – but not being seen can certainly allow clients to relax and make good use of sessions. At the beginning of the session, some clients tell me that they are making themselves comfortable, maybe that they are covered by a blanket or are curling up on the sofa. This can also be the way a client provides themselves and me with a 'verbal arrival' to a session. How a client arrives to phone session is significant and will be explored later.

Grumet's (1979) review and case report on phone therapy gives a good overview of the differences and advantages to the medium. Grumet noticed that the visual privacy of the phone allows the 'reluctant or ambivalent patient to achieve closeness and a feeling of safety at a distance'. He found it particularly significant that his patients who felt shame and embarrassment were better able to approach their feelings without having to see their therapist's facial reactions. Grumet said that the phone allows his patients to maintain a sense of control over the process of therapy. 'A prospective patient is able to test the waters and can dispel some of the mystique of therapy at a safe distance'. Grumet also found many clients said that they were less inhibited and guarded when they were relaxed in their own environment. He noted that what clothing was worn and the general appearance of either party had no impact on the therapeutic work and concluded that 'the telephone offers a strategic combination of intimacy and safety and is a useful treatment option'.

Anonymity, equality and client participation

Aftel and Tolmach Lakoff (1985), whose research focused on working with young people in urban areas, found that without sight, an increased sense of anonymity was also shown to be beneficial. Their feedback showed that the intimacy of face-to-face therapy caused some young people intolerable anxiety.

When thinking about specific client groups, working on the phone can be really useful to young people and college or university students. So, often, it is assumed that Generation Z are willing or comfortable only with communication by video. Just because talking face time on video or indeed messaging might be a more usual way for young people to communicate with each other, I don't think it necessarily follows that this is the preferred medium by which to have therapy. My experience of working with young people face to face, via video and on the phone has shown that more clients than I had originally imagined find it easier to communicate without being seen, especially when they're talking about embarrassing or difficult issues such as gender identity, sexual problems and sexual abuse.

The absence of visual co-presence is definitely helpful to some clients. My clients and those of therapists who have contributed to this book have reported this to be their experience. Some of my clients express the benefit of visual anonymity by telling me that it feels easier to talk when they don't see me. Like Grumet's patients, my clients quite regularly present with shame-related issues often experienced by mothers who live apart from their children. Shame and guilt are accompanied by painful fear of judgement which forms part of our work. I believe that for clients not being seen allows for greater expression and flow. This, together with a non-judgement and empathy expressed compassionately through the therapist's effective use of voice, results in the positive outcomes described by Grumet.

On the phone, the medium for therapy becomes a space for greater equality between client and therapist. Thought-provoking views on this are shared by other therapists in this book, particularly those discussing equality, diversity and inclusion in Chapter 7. I will always endeavour to talk with the client about the impact of a difficult session, grounding them where necessary, but the client knows they have the easier option of ending the call rather than having to leave the therapist's room when they have phone therapy. This makes therapy more equitable and allows the client greater control. Perhaps, this is a challenge for therapists at times and is something to bear in mind when we work with hearing alone.

Lesley Murdin, a psychoanalytic psychotherapist whose paper considers the ways in which the telephone resembles the use of the couch, concurs. 'Once the telephone connection is made, communication may be easier, allowing shameful secrets to be told while there is the possibility of simply putting the phone down' (Murdin, 2021). While acknowledging caveats to the use of the couch and the phone, Murden concludes that the phone 'brings a person back to his or her own thoughts and associations, in some cases more effectively than sitting in a chair opposite the therapist' (Murdin, 2021).

In addition to enhanced feelings of safety and equality, Day and Schneider (2002) suggest that this finding may be related to increased patient efforts to communicate when they aren't in the same room with the therapist. In a comparison of face-to-face, video and audio therapy, Day and Schneider found that patients participated significantly more actively in both audio and video sessions than they did in the face-to-face setting.

What about silence? It's important to remember that although the phone can provide ease of communication for clients, there is also a need for the work of therapy to ebb as well as flow. We know that silence is needed, and this can be experienced extremely powerfully on the phone. How we manage silence is included in the core phone counselling discussed in the next chapter.

Phone therapy's benefits to therapists

Although the best interest of the client is our main priority, I think it is important to remember that working via the phone has benefits for therapists too. To name just a few – the convenience of not needing access to a therapy room and pay room hire fees, flexibility to schedule sessions earlier or later in the day as there is no travel time to consider, a greater sense of ease and comfort which comes from not needing to be mindful of being seen.

Over the years, I have trained and supervised therapists and heard many accounts from practitioners sharing the benefits of working with voice alone. These include being able to move about the room during a session to ease back pain which had ended the ability to continue working face to face. Therapists feeling liberated by knowing that clients would never know that they are wheelchair users. Being able to discharge feelings and tension by scrunching up facial muscles without being seen. Not needing to consider how our face looks, allowing ourselves to frown, smile and be unconcerned about whether an eyebrow is raised, all of which can allow us to focus less on ourselves and more fully on the client.

Main differences between phone and face-to-face therapy

Further information on how to manage the differences discussed here can be found in relevant areas of this book. As a snapshot to help define phone therapy, here are the main characteristics of differences.

Client unfamiliarity with phone therapy boundaries

Boundary matters and the therapeutic frame included at the beginning of this chapter needs to be thought through by practitioners and explained to clients as they might not understand the differences between face-to-face therapy and phone therapy. It is the role of the therapist to explain what phone therapy is, that you are a qualified practitioner who offers therapy via the phone, how this differs from a helpline and other matters usually included in a phone therapy contract. I believe it is the therapist's job to develop competence on the phone, gain confidence in the medium and communicate this to clients before the first session and during the work. If therapists believe that phone therapy is as valid and effective as face-to-face therapy, there is a good chance the client will experience this to be true.

Assessment and contracting

Independent practitioners and therapy services need to review processes, procedures and policies and adapt them for phone therapy. Contracts might be sent to clients in advance and how agreement and consent will be obtained, will need to be considered when both parties are not in the same room, for example, the client's signature. Assessment sessions might include gathering information in advance of a first appointment by use of questionnaires in formats that don't require both parties to be physically present. Both contracting and assessment questions and information need to be adapted and provision made to safeguard the client when working at a distance. This includes a robust assessment, clarity about limits to confidentiality and agreement about what environment is private enough for therapy.

Not being physically present in times of emergency

Thought needs to be given to how client risk and emergencies will be managed. This is best done in advance so that it can be acted upon should an emergency arise. Clarity about limits to confidentiality, consent to hold and contact a named person in times of emergency, creation of a workable emergency procedure or flow chart are helpful and will include the use of a second phone, emergency services numbers, how any waiting clients will be contacted and what actions might need to occur after the crisis has passed.

Phone therapy can be quicker in pace

Without seeing, the phone can allow clients to disclose information more quickly than the average face-to-face session. It is possible for clients to feel safer without seeing their therapist or being seen and for early, deep disclosure to take place. Trust can be built quickly on the phone, sometimes in the first or early sessions. The combination of client pace together with a lot of material and the intimacy created by channelling through the sense of hearing means that some clients may experience difficulty processing the session. This is important to monitor and there are ways of helping the client if this occurs which will be covered later. There are advantages to the speed of session. Clients sometimes tell me that they can't believe how much we have addressed in a session. It's possible for clients to feel understood earlier on in the work, engaging more quickly in the therapy.

Working without body language

Therapists might feel anxiety about not being able to see the client's body language and feel concerned that they will get drawn into believing all that the client says and get caught up in the client's denial or fantasy. In my experience, the pace of the work, checking assumptions and gently challenging the client can make up for this. It's important to clarify what feels skimmed over or not making sense.

Potentially more distractions and interruptions

Without the relative assurance of a therapy room there is the possibility for breaches of privacy. The sudden lockdown due to COVID-19 pandemic resulted in unprepared phone therapists as well as clients, which if the circumstances weren't so traumatic, could be humorous as make-shift therapeutic environments ranged from garden sheds to being incorporated into permitted daily exercise. Therapists need to be explicit when discussing the importance of privacy and help clients, particularly young people create a safe enough therapeutic space for sessions. Highlighting distractions such as reading messages and multitasking also needs to be discussed and negotiated with clients.

Lack of transition time

How a phone session begins and ends needs to be thought through and managed well by therapists. The click of a phone line going dead abruptly after a quick goodbye can feel rejecting for clients. When clients leave at the end of a face-to-face session, they have time to gather themselves and their belongings as they step out into life beyond the therapy room. Taking steps to help clients to end phone sessions, particularly difficult ones, compensates for the lack of transition time and needs to be considered in the context of the therapist's modality and setting.

We will consider how we will bring these and other matters to the client's attention. Some are about how we contract with clients; others are to do with how we work with them. Clarity and preparation help therapists and clients feel confident in the medium.

References

Aftel, M., & Tolmach Lakoff, R. (1985). *When talk is not cheap*. Grand Central Publications.

BACP Online and Phone Therapy (OPT) competence framework. (2021). www.bacp. co.uk/media/10849/bacp-online-and-phone-therapy-competence-framework-feb21.pdf

Brenes, G. A., Ingram, C. W., & Danhauer, S. C. (2012). Telephone-delivered psychotherapy for late-life anxiety. *Psychological Services, 9*(2), 219–220. https://doi.org/10.1037/a0025950

Day, S. X., & Schneider, P. L. (2002). Psychotherapy using distance technology: A comparison of face-to-face, video, and audio treatment. *Journal of Counseling Psychology, 49*(4), 499–503. https://doi.org/10.1037/0022-0167.49.4.499

de Leo, D., Buono, M. D., & Dwyer, J. (2002). Suicide among the elderly: The long-term impact of a telephone support and assessment intervention in northern Italy. *British Journal of Psychiatry, 181*(3), 226–229. https://doi.org/10.1192/bjp.181.3.226

Grumet, G. W. (1979). Telephone therapy: A review and case report. *American Journal of Orthopsychiatry, 49*(4), 574–584. https://doi.org/10.1111/j.1939-0025.1979.tb02643.x

Lynch, D. J., Tamburrino, M. B., & Nagel, R. (1997). Telephone counseling for patients with minor depression: Preliminary findings in a family practice setting. *The Journal of Family Practice, 44*(3), 293–298.

Murdin, L. (2021). Is anyone there? Use of the telephone and use of the couch. *British Journal of Psychotherapy, 37*(2), 234–243. https://doi.org/10.1111/bjp.12629

Reese, R. J., Conoley, C. W., & Brossart, D. F. (2002). Effectiveness of telephone counseling: A field-based investigation. *Journal of Counseling Psychology, 49*(2), 233–242. https://doi.org/10.1037/0022-0167.49.2.233

Reese, R. J., Conoley, C. W., & Brossart, D. F. (2006). The attractiveness of telephone counseling: An empirical investigation of client perceptions. *Journal of Counseling & Development, 84*(1), 54–60. https://doi.org/10.1002/j.1556-6678.2006.tb00379.x

Spizman. (2001). *Is counseling by telephone effective?* Doctoral Thesis, University of Pennsylvania.

Suler, J. (2004). The online disinhibition effect. *Cyber Psychology & Behavior, 7*(3), 321–326. https://doi.org/10.1089/1094931041291295

Swinson, R. P., Fergus, K. D., Cox, B. J., & Wickwire, K. (1995). Efficacy of telephone-administered behavioral therapy for panic disorder with agoraphobia. *Behaviour Research and Therapy, 33*(4), 465–469. https://doi.org/10.1016/0005-7967(94)00061-n

Chapter 3

Communication and core phone therapy skills

Phone therapy calls for the ability to listen deeply. Also, it requires us to respond in a thought through, timely way. Channelling information through one sense alone, our hearing is heightened. We can trust our ears unless perhaps we have a hearing impediment, but even so, heightened hearing isn't the same as heightened listening. In the absence of seeing, we need to learn to listen out for far more than is needed in a face-to-face session and we need to respond differently too. This requires significantly more of our attention than having a chat on the phone or even a business call.

Non-verbal communication and paralanguage

Communicating by sound is multi-layered and provides much more information than what first meets the eye or ear for that matter. Conversations do not only consist of spoken words, but they also include non-verbal vocalisations which occur most often in spontaneous, conversational dialogue, as opposed to a pre-pared lecture or speech. Paralanguage, a term coined by the American linguist George Trager (1958), is the study of vocal signals and voice modification over and above words that we use to communicate meaning. Some paralanguage researchers include body language cues too and as Peter Matthews (2014) says, 'The boundaries of paralanguage are (unavoidably) imprecise'. As phone therapy is concerned with voice and hearing without sight, our focus will be on what our clients say, how they say it, as well as the communication that occurs far beyond the words they speak. Our client's choice of words, along with their gasps, sighs, throat clearing, whispers, shouts, laughter, crying, speeding up, slowing down and being completely silent – gives us a wealth of information about who they are, their experiences and emotional state.

Vocal characteristics – pitch, tone and intonation

The sound of someone's voice is as unique to them as how they look but even so, vocal characteristics fall into the following categories.

DOI: 10.4324/9781003253396-3

Pitch is the highness or lowness of a person's vocal tone. As outlined in Chapter 1, frequency measures the cycle rate of a sound wave and pitch is how high or low it sounds when you hear it. The smaller the larynx the higher the pitch which is why women tend to have higher voices than men. We might notice when a man has a higher pitch. Political scientist Casey Klofstad (2016) examined how vocal perceptions influence decision-making and found that in Western cultures, lower pitches are viewed favourably for both men and women in terms of strength, dominance and electability. A case in point is British Prime Minister Margaret Thatcher, who had voice coaching to make her voice sound lower and more commanding. Klofstad found that low is generally preferred in a leader, but the question up for debate is whether they actually are a better leader. Interestingly, higher pitches were preferred in East Asian countries, which illustrates the importance of context and interpretation when we work with clients. As phone therapists, it is useful to notice how we respond to clients with high or low pitch, what assumptions we might be making about them, particularly about gender identity, race, culture and disability.

Tone is the quality in the voice, how the speaker feels about the person they are communicating with. Think about how much meaning there is in the phrase 'I didn't like his tone of voice'. The emotional impact of communication isn't so much what is said but how it is said. Imagine listening to a fire officer being interviewed at the scene of a fire. If their tone is even and their words are calmly delivered, we listen on one level, interpreting what the words mean. But if they say the same words and their voice breaks with emotion, our empathy rises. Horowitz (2012, p. 129) writes about the flow of tones known as prosody, which Charles Darwin believed were the evolutionary precursor of human language. Horowitz says that neural imaging and EEG studies have demonstrated that prosody is not processed in the speech comprehension area, known as Wernicke's region of the brain, but in the right hemisphere, in the region more important for emotional processing. A client's tone can move us very deeply on the phone. In return, our heartfelt empathy will be conveyed very profoundly to our client via our tone of voice.

Intonation is the variety, melody or inflection of a person's voice. Beyond the individual's use of voice, their intonation refers to the music of the language they speak, that is how it rises and falls over a chunk of speech – a sentence, phrase, group of sentences. Each language has its own intonation, some are more musical than others, and in English, a wide range is used. Intonation can be rising, falling or flat and is used to communicate how a speaker feels.

Uptalk

Uptalk, also known as upspeak and high-rising terminal (HRT), is a speech pattern in which phrases and sentences habitually end with a rising intonation as if the statement were a question. It's been suggested that uptalk has a facilitative function in conversation. It encourages the addressee to participate in the conversation as rising intonation asks a question. Ending a sentence with a rising intonation can also subtly indicate that the speaker is 'not finished yet', perhaps discouraging interruption (Allen, 1990; Guy et al., 1986; Warren, 2005).

Various theories abound about the origins of universally used uptalk, including that it's Australian (think about the soap opera Neighbours), that started in Scandinavia, Japan and that it's Celtic as well as Bristolian. You might notice that more women use uptalk than men and until fairly recently, it was thought that women have a greater influence on language change, using uptalk in particular. However, it seems that in the light of current social constructionist understandings of gender, this is changing (Cameron, 2003).

Why is uptalk relevant to phone therapy? Consider how this might influence you. Beyond perhaps being irritating, you could feel less inclined to interject because uptalk covertly implies that the speaker has not finished yet. As a client's use of uptalk asks a question, you might feel drawn to answer them when a question is not actually being asked, particularly as it is sometimes regarded as a lack of confidence, as the speaker is looking for reassurance or confirmation. Rob Drummond (2014), a lecturer in linguistics at Manchester Metropolitan University, feels differently.

> A lot of people think it's a sign of insecurity and being unsure, but I think it's misunderstood. It's used in such a variety of ways, yes it can be that, but it can also be used quite aggressively and in a dominating way.

When a client uses uptalk, I try to see past the general use of rising inflection and consider their individual circumstances. Are they insecure and wanting answers or am I feeling controlled? Sometimes, a therapist's use of uptalk has an impact when I train groups on the phone. I find it interesting to hear the reaction of others in the group, some therapists clearly feeling obligated to respond. In some instances, if it was left unacknowledged it can cause interruption. That said, a client might use uptalk as a trendy way of talking, particularly if they're young which brings us to another popular way voice can be used.

Vocal fry or creaking voice

Vocal fry is when the voice sounds raspy or creaky and occurs when there is not enough breath being pushed through the vocal cords. Without enough air, vocal cords can't rub together to create a clear sound. Instead, they create a creaky, hollow, rattling noise at the bottom of the vocal register. I've heard it said that vocal fry imitates the voice of smokers and marijuana users who hold their breath and speak at the same time. The inference here is that it's perceived as cool, and if celebrity use of vocal fry is anything to go by, we shouldn't be surprised that it's a particularly popular use of paralanguage.

What about the impact of accents, colloquialisms, cultural differences and disabilities on voice? The anxiety of not being able to understand a client on the phone is often discussed when I train therapists, and we will consider these matters in greater detail in Chapter 7. For now, being mindful of intonation can help when working with clients for whom English is not their first language. If their language does not have the same range, I have heard clients from some cultural backgrounds being described by therapists as sounding like they were monotonous or even bored when speaking English, when they're not. Awareness of equality, diversity and inclusion (EDI) should sit at the heart of every practitioner's work, and we need to consider how we make EDI integral to our phone therapy practice too.

A client might have a flat, monotonous sounding intonation or tone if they are nervous or more introverted in temperament, more on this in a while. There can be other reasons that lead therapists to imagine issues that are not so.

> *I once had a client who at her first session sounded flat, low in tone and spoke very softly. I had known that she had suffered from postpartum depression and listening to her voice, I imagined she was still experiencing this. Knowing that I needed to keep my mind's eye in check, I discussed my impression of her tone and that I wondered whether she was perhaps still suffering from depression. At this, my client became immediately animated in intonation and assured me that this was not the case. She went on to explain that she was trying to speak as softly and quietly as possible as she didn't want to be overheard by others in the house. Having a clear understanding of the way in which she was communicating, we discussed how she might find a more private space for her sessions.*

Not making assumptions cannot be overemphasised when we work on the phone. Without checking with the client, I might have projected a protracted medical condition on to her.

The therapist's voice

While understanding the client is of concern for some, other therapists are worried about whether they will be understood by their clients. Obviously, we have to work with the voice we are born with and the accent or dialect we have learnt from the family and community in which we live. Even so, with awareness therapists can adapt the characteristics of their voices and use pitch, tone and intonation more effectively than in the therapy room where body language and facial expression can be used as compensation. Maxine Rosenfield (1997) writes that 'with practice, therapists should develop an upbeat, professional counselling tone' to avoid a mechanical overly sweet or corporate voice.

Our first contact with clients is crucial. Exploring how we use our voices in addition to what we say is worthy of inclusion later when we consider the initial session. The starting point is knowing that just like you, clients will be consciously and unconsciously picking up on every nuance of your voice. Taking time to reflect on your 'phone voice' and the ways in which this differs from your 'phone therapist voice' is important. Better still, get feedback from a therapist colleague. My trainings include core skills practice sessions with others on the course and therapists find that there is rich learning from both therapist and client roles.

Warm and welcoming

In addition to warm and welcoming words, mirroring this stance in your voice can be achieved by centring yourself before the call, relaxing your body, shoulders and neck particularly, to avoid constricting the muscles around the larynx. Taking time to sit comfortably and breathing into your diaphragm can help avoid a strained or tight voice, breathy or hoarse voice, feeling the need to clear or that there's a lump in the throat.

Lowering the pitch and adopting an open, prepared and emotionally available tone will help put the client at tease. Show some degree of variation in your intonation, the rise and fall of your voice. When I train on the phone, I have noticed that therapists can sound flat when they're anxious. Watch your tempo or speed of talking. Pace yourself, without seeing face to face you might lose or confuse a client if you speak too quickly. Watch your volume. Talking loudly and directly into your client's ear will overwhelm them.

Without a doubt, clients will notice changes in your voice beyond the words. As you gain confidence, you will be able to use your voice to show understanding and empathy, moving adeptly with the client. There will be times when you'll speak softly, gently, slowly striking the right note with a client at a moment of heartfelt emotional expression. When this passes, you will pick up pace and project your voice once more to mirror the client's process.

The effective therapeutic phone alliance

BACP OPT competence framework (2021) states that we need to form and maintain an effective therapeutic alliance, use effective language and communication processes and we need to work with an awareness of and mitigating against the increased risk of misunderstanding when communicating in online and phone therapy.

Whether the client phones you, or you phone the client, the first contact will be encountering each other's voices. As we know that clients are likely to feel vulnerable, anxious and distressed, just as when face to face, the therapist's role is to help put the client at ease for the client to feel secure and accepted. Whatever your theoretical orientation, demonstrating empathy and understanding is one of the ways we start to develop rapport.

Without sight, this can feel a difficult task for some therapists indeed Antonioni (1973) noted that counsellors reported feelings of inferiority or inadequacy when working on the phone, feeling that part of the person was missing or that they wanted more visual cues to assess patients' reactions. By contrast, Antonioni highlighted a gap between the apparently effective communication of empathy via telephone as rated by patients and the counsellors' own perceptions that the phone detrimentally affects the interaction. We can take heart that the patients in this study had little problem receiving the counsellor's empathic communication. It is certainly my experience that clients are able to sense empathy and understanding without sight and that alliance building is just as achievable when working with voice alone.

Demonstrating empathy without body language and physical presence

On the phone, as clients aren't able to read your facial expression or body language, your physical presence will mean nothing to them, and you can't hand them a tissue. We have to listen deeply to what is being said and not said, sensing our client before audibly communicating empathy.

It might help us to consider Carl Roger's belief that empathy was a process not a state. Redefining his description of empathy in 1975, he said

> It includes communicating your senses of his/her world as you look with fresh and unfrightened eyes at elements of which the individual is frightened. It means frequently checking with him/her as to the accuracy of your sensings and being guided by the responses you receive.
>
> (Rogers, 1975, p. 3)

How you communicate empathy and understanding will differ as you work within each client's individual frame of reference and your theoretical orientation, but key elements of verbally demonstrating empathy are likely to include the following.

Verbal nods

In the absence of being able to nod or use other body language signals, paralanguage and encouragers like 'uh-huh', 'mmm', 'yes', 'no', 'I see', 'right' and other verbal signals show that you're engaged in listening to the client. When it comes to forming and developing the therapeutic alliance, Bedi (2006) and Bedi and Duff (2014), who studied patient-rated importance of various factors, demonstrated that while eye contact is one of the most important elements, non-verbal gestures and body language were rated as significantly less import than patients being validated by their therapist. Bedi (2006) listed validation as therapists 'normalizing the patient's experience, framing it as reasonable or understandable, identifying and reflecting back feelings, paraphrasing, agreeing, and making encouraging and comments. Significantly, none of these are reliant on visual co-presence'.

This research shows the positive impact of audible validation, the value of it to our clients which has perhaps been underestimated by therapists when comparing it to body language. That said, in the absence of non-verbal gestures and body language, we need to assess and tune into what our clients need from us. Although we will use more of these than we might in a face-to-face session, the aim of verbal or audible nods is of course to make them unobtrusive so as not to interrupt the client's thoughts and encourage them to say more. We show we are listening and don't mean to interrupt by giving back-channel signals as they are also known. Macaulay (2006) writes that back-channelling with *uh-huhs*, *mhm* and other brief comments communicates that the speaker is not trying to take over the flow or take turns; in fact, they allow for the reverse, as these are indications that we expect the speaker to continue.

Attuning yourself to the client is important, too many audible nods will obstruct a client's flow. A phone therapist told me that she was at great pains not to sound like a mooing cow to her clients. That said, too little audible communication from us can lead clients to feel rejection or abandonment. This means we will be tuning in, taking our lead from each client and some will need more communication lubricants, as I call them, than others. A client tailing off might indicate that you haven't got the balance right and a client saying 'Hello, are you still there?' is a definite indicator that they need more paralanguage and encouragers from you.

Maintaining contact – fast talkers

Pete Sanders (2007) states that to maintain contact we need to encourage the client to say more and reflect the content of their statements, sometimes interrupting them, perhaps when they are in full flow. I agree that learning to be comfortable with interrupting the client to slow them down on occasion is essential, particularly when there is a lot of material. Some clients are fast talkers and the pace of the work without sight intensifies this, alongside the impact of disinhibition. When clients are fast, distressed or sounding confused, in addition to clarifying by reflecting back or paraphrasing, you can use your tone and pace to help them reflect and for you to get a better understanding. I think that without visual cues it is possible for clients to have difficulty processing material or feel very emotional and alone with their distress, which is why sometimes a more interactive approach is needed.

Interestingly, Day and Schneider (2002), who researched client participation in distance modes, found that patients participated significantly more actively in both of the distance modes (audio and video) than they did in the face-to-face setting. They suggested that this finding may be related to increased patient efforts to communicate when they weren't in the room with the therapist or to an enhanced sense of 'safety' engendered by a distance mode like the phone.

An adult client who had had face-to-face therapy before starting sessions with me would regularly say that she was ready to end her sessions before the hour was up. She would say that she had enough to process for that week. Unlike avoidance, she experienced this as feeling full, she wanted to end early and reflect on her own until the following week. She remarked on this difference, and we discussed it as she had not experienced the need to end early when in face-to-face therapy. Perhaps she had increased her efforts to communicate on the phone, maybe she felt safer, but it was clear that the phone allowed for a faster, fuller session.

My rule of thumb for verbally communicating, interrupt a client or allowing flow is relative to:

1   How much you tend to verbally interact with clients now – this will depend on your theoretical orientation and your counselling style – if you are largely quiet, relying on body language and your presence, it's likely you will need to communicate verbally more often when you work on the phone.
2   The amount of material brought to the session – are either you or the client becoming confused?
3   The level of distress your client is experiencing. Reflective silence aside, I might connect more with a highly distressed client.
4   The client's experience of therapy generally. Have they experienced phone therapy before?

Making and maintaining contact with less communicative clients

What about clients who say very little or remain quiet? Feeling different to silences that we know are necessary for client reflection, this can be a source of considerable discomfort and anxiety for therapists. Left unexplored and without seeing the client, fantasies about what they are thinking of you the therapist, feeling inadequate or de-skilled and all manner of difficult countertransference issues can take hold. Know that you might find a quiet client challenging, and when you encounter this, take note of how you are feeling and the ways you might try to rectify this and encourage greater flow. I tend to notice anxiety about a client's silence in my body first, a tension in my shoulders and neck followed by a desire to fill the space to avoid my unease and the imagined or otherwise discomfort of my client. Also, I become aware that I am working hard, trying to engage my client. In my practice, clients who say very little tend to be the young people I work with as an employee of a counselling service charity, rather than adults.

Client reservation might be due to a number of reasons, perhaps shyness, lack of privacy or reluctance to have therapy. An exploration in supervision before discussing with the client your impressions of how they are presenting and how you are working together should help. Working on the phone requires a collaborative approach, and this together with allowing time to build trust and develop the relationship is likely to pave the way for the work to continue on the phone. My experience of clients with whom I have not managed to develop a therapeutic alliance has tended to be young people whose parents have wanted them to have therapy rather than themselves. Just as when this occurs in the face-to-face setting, working in these circumstances is rarely successful.

Personality type

Another perspective for considering how to develop an effective alliance on the phone is through the lens of psychological types described by C. G. Jung and developed by Myers-Briggs into Myers-Briggs Type Indicator, which describes 16 distinctive personality types. Jung used the words introvert and extrovert differently to how they are often used today where the term extroverted is outgoing, social, and charismatic and introverted is shy and withdrawn. Jung described the preferred focus of extroverts is to direct their energy to the outer world and that introverts orientate their energy to their inner world – both perfectly valid and healthy differences in personality style. It's not my intention to put people in boxes or label them, but it can be useful to consider how extroversion and introversion can present on the phone.

As a client on the phone, an extrovert might sound loud, flamboyant, bombastic, perhaps even a little manic without visuals to give you the whole picture. Sometimes, it is difficult to get a word in when you are face to face with an extrovert – so imagine what it could be like when they gain momentum and they can't read your body language. It's sometimes necessary to interrupt an extrovert to check meaning, slow them down to aid reflection. As extroverts often speak to process thoughts, they might be more likely to experience disinhibition on the phone.

An introvert, on the other hand, is a client who might be more softly spoken, measured, reflective, could sound depressed when they aren't, they could sound repressed, cool, uninterested, offhand or even critical when they are not. Again, without body language, be mindful not to make assumptions. I notice that I check meaning more often to avoid fantasy and countertransference as much as possible. It's also worth bearing in mind that an introvert might not make much sound when they cry.

Recognising emotions through the client's paralanguage

As we gain confidence in the medium of the phone and come to trust that it is possible to work without seeing the client, we'll come to experience the rich harvest of each individual client's vocal characteristics. We notice uptalk, vocal fry, gasping, murmuring, giggling, fast talking, slowing down and get curious about what this means. Paying attention, we notice when a client's usual paralanguage changes and we work with this.

> *In one session, I noticed my client releasing a number of sighs. This was particularly apparent to me as she was typically a fast, free flowing talker. When I remarked on her sighs, she exclaimed that she wasn't able to hide anything from me, that it was just as well that we weren't in the same room as I'd be picking up on all sorts of things that I wasn't able to see. In spite of this being an intriguing response – her experience of not being seen which part of me would have loved to explore – I chose to focus on the sigh. Our discussion was an important turning point in the work, her sigh signalled her shift from resignation of her circumstances to a place of acceptance.*

Crying

Keep your ear cocked for crying – some clients cry very, very quietly. Crying can take you by surprise; so listen out for pitch, tone and pace changes that might signal that a client is about to cry. Slow down, tune in and use empathy and identification if you suspect or expect there are likely to be tears. I might say something along the lines of 'I image it's really hard to acknowledge that . . . or . . . that is really very moving to hear that'. Stop talking when you realise a client is crying. What we try to avoid is anything from us that inhibits the client or might inadvertently indicate that it's not ok for them to cry. I sometimes use paralanguage instead of words, a soft, 'mmm' in a low tone or a soft 'ok'. Just as when face to face, a client might apologise to which we can verbally normalise and demonstrate acceptance. Some clients might tell you that they are crying softly.

> *I had a client who verbally described how she cried while she was crying. She was in the midst of deep grief work, coming to terms with being estranged from her child, which she experienced as a living bereavement. She would tell me that if I saw her, I'd see that she had tears streaming down her face. It was important for her to describe the emotion as well as express it and it was just as important that I received this description, accepting and acknowledging her pain.*

If you were face to face, you would probably hand the client a tissue. On the phone you'll need to hand your client what is known as a virtual tissue, which means to use words to let them know it is ok to cry and you are with them. So, you'd say something like, 'I can hear how hard this is for you or how much that hurt you'.

Weeping loudly can feel hard to deal with when you first work on the phone, particularly with new clients who aren't familiar to us. Your ear is flooded with intense upset, perhaps during a first or early session while you are still assessing risk – it can feel startling. Remember the research of Melanie Aeschlimann et al. (2008), who studied emotional expression and hearing (Chapter 1). Sounds that evoke the greatest emotional response in us are those that are made by humans and those with negative emotional responses as they are perceived as louder, even when they were at the same amplitude as other sounds. Take your time when a client cries. Assure them that there is no rush. They might need to blow their nose too, which could mean they put down the phone if they're holding it, or you might experience an earful of blowing if they're using earphones.

We need to give full permission for crying by not interfering too much, but they do need something from you so that when the moment has passed, they don't feel shame, embarrassment or that you've been overwhelmed by them. Listen out for when the client begins to move on and adjust your tone, volume and speed accordingly.

Silences

Silences on the phone require wider consideration and can cause therapists anxiety when they're new to the medium or when starting work with a new client. Indeed, Christogiorgos et al. (2010) affirm that silence from the patient can leave therapists unclear about the meaning of a silence or unsure about when to allow space for a 'skilful silence'.

During phone therapy, a client's silence can be for a number of reasons, including reflection, rejection, distraction, privacy breach or simply having a sip of tea. While we wait, all of these potential scenarios need to be considered, including the fact that using our hearing sense alone to assess a silence heightens our emotional vigilance. As discussed in Chapter 1, a lack of sound increases our attention and arousal, increasing our ear's sensitivity, warning our brain that something is amiss which is part of the reason silences on the phone can feel uncomfortable (Horowitz, 2012).

Each client's silence will be different, and it takes a while to get to know their rhythms.

Allowing the client space for reflection is essential, so manage your discomfort. If you sense that the silence is being used by the client to process feelings or thoughts, say nothing. Depending on the client, the stage of the work and your modality, you might decide to offer something to assure the client that it's fine for them to be silent for a while or maintain connection to the client by saying that you are still there. When I feel I need to connect I prefer a transparent approach, saying that I've noticed that they have been quiet for a while and that I'm still there.

If you hear crying, you're likely to want to respond and acknowledge this. There is no one way of working with this, and some therapists are keen to know how long they should leave a silence before speaking again. It's likely that because a lack of sound heightens our arousal, sitting with a client's silence feels longer on the phone. Rosenfield (1997, p. 26) writes 'A 10-second silence can feel more like 30 seconds and a 30-second silence more like a few minutes'. I agree, silences definitely seem longer without sight. Sanders (2007) says that he's found speaking every 15–45 seconds feels about the right period of time to leave a client silence. I won't usually leave a silence during a first session. After this, I watch the clock when a silence starts. Depending on the length of our relationship, the issue the client is focusing on and the stage of the work, I sometimes leave a silence for anywhere between 20 seconds and around two minutes before saying anything. The more familiar the client is with therapy and if their awareness of their process is high – the longer I leave a silence.

A new client of mine who had had quite a bit of therapy before would settle into quite long periods of silence which I felt were pertinent, full and reflective. My sense was not to jump in but to wait even though we didn't know each other very well. After a few weeks she said, 'These silences really help me to digest what we talk about'. In addition to feeling pleased that she could take and make use of silence, the experience for me was a lesson in intuiting the client's needs and trusting the value of attention and listening deeply to what is said and not said.

That said, therapy without a therapist's physical presence can on occasion feel stark, too much in the void in which some clients feel alone and on occasion rejected by the therapist. Reeves (2015) raises the point that some silences which are experienced as therapeutic when working face to face can make patients feel like their therapist has disappeared or deserted them. Remember, a lack of sound will raise arousal levels in clients too, possibly warning the brain that something is amiss, alerting them that something potentially bad is about to happen. Be mindful of what you last said to a client and at what point the silence occurred. Your theoretical orientation will guide your response; however, take time to consider how you might need to adapt your modality and style when you work on the phone, particularly if your approach usually allows for long silences and minimal interpretations or reflections from the therapist.

Other reasons for silences include clients who stop talking because someone has walked into the room or another type of privacy breach. Clients might lapse into silence because they become distracted by something in their environment, a text message for example or they are unable to talk because they are drinking or eating. These contracting and boundary matters are explored in other chapters.

Anger

A client's expression of anger can be a difficult experience when we work on the phone for different reasons. As we channel what the client says through one sense alone, our ear, a sudden, loud outburst is likely to take us by surprise and on an evolutionary level, triggering fear within us. Without visual cues, a tirade of anger, especially with a new client can be unnerving. In my experience, angry clients in denial can be tricky. Those who don't take responsibility for their circumstances or think they are 'right', or the injured party can feel like a machine gun, stating their case. Phone therapy can be faster paced than face to face and without being able to see your responses, it can be easier for clients to express full throttle anger as they can't see you trying to interject. Anger might also be expressed earlier in the work than when working face to face because the relationship can develop faster without being physically present. Therapists sometimes fear a client putting phone down in anger. I've not had this experience, and I think this is probably because I offer contracted, pre-booked counselling sessions. I imagine that therapists who work on crisis lines and helplines which receive ad hoc calls are more likely to experience a caller putting the phone down, perhaps when frustrated, or if interrupted or when they have received enough from the call.

If anger on the phone worries you, remind yourself that anger in the therapy room can be just as challenging, perhaps more so at times as you can see your client raging and the client might see flickers of disapproval, anger, or fear cross your face. We know that anger can be useful as well as damaging and different types of anger can range from a temporary emotional expression, a reaction to a trigger or it might be a client's general state, perhaps the presenting issue. Whether on the phone or face to face, anger can be difficult to respond to therapeutically, it can go against our intention to be compassionate, accepting and understanding. It's easy for us to take a client's anger personally and as empathy saps away, we can feel incompetent, de-skilled, frustrated, impotent. We might have an urge to express our own anger, withdraw or act passive aggressively, particularly if disinhibition is activated within us.

Supervision is crucial. How you will respond on the phone will depend on your theoretical orientation and how the anger was expressed. Was it a clear expression, an open attack, passive aggressive or sarcastic? What if anything was your part? What was triggered in you? On the phone, not responding to a client's anger can be received as uncaring, critical or abandoning. In supervision, examine with emotional honesty how you might stay connected and explore anger with a client, how you can bear a client's anger without freezing or attacking back.

Both Rosenfield (1997) and Sanders (2007) discuss good boundary setting including what therapists would consider behaviour that they are not prepared to tolerate. I agree and think that there are no hard and fast rules, that it is a matter for each practitioner to reflect on individually, alongside organisational policy and procedure if you work for a therapy service.

In addition to other emotions, one clear reason for anger to be more easily expressed on the phone by clients and therapists alike is the psychological phenomenon of disinhibition.

Psychological processes and disinhibition

The BACP OPT competence framework (2021) states that we need to have the ability to work remotely with psychological processes. In particular, we need 'knowledge of certain phenomena affecting self-presentation relating to identity and telepresence' (this means that people may present themselves and experience others differently when they are unseen or online). In my experience, the key phenomena affecting self-presentation relating to phone therapy are invisibility, lowered inhibitions, increased possibility of fantasy, speculation, projection, transference and countertransference. These phenomena and psychological processes are further explored in the following chapter. Also, we need to 'manage the impact of disinhibition by drawing on knowledge that people may behave differently remotely to the ways in which they might interact when in-the-room' (2021).

John Suler's (2004) paper 'The Online Disinhibition Effect' sets out how some people self-disclose more easily and readily online. When they feel they're at a distance, their psychological barriers can weaken, they feel braver, making it easier to express themselves, particularly negative comments.

What does this mean for phone therapy? Although written with an online (text, email and video) focus, it can be useful to consider the six factors which Suler cites as leading to the weakening of psychological barrier in cyberspace and how this might apply to phone therapy clients.

Dissasociative anonymity – when people are able to hide some or all of their identity, having no name or not using their real name. Even though anonymity is removed by knowing each other's identity, an inability to physically see someone can cause inhibitions to be lowered which could occur on the phone.

Invisibility – not being seen online, not having to worry about how the other looks (or sounds) in response to what they have said. Invisibility is particularly relevant to phone therapy.

Asynchronicity – when people don't communicate in real time (i.e. posting online), they don't have to face someone's immediate reaction, described as 'emotional hit and run' (K. Munro, unpublished observations, 2003).

Solipsistic introjections – in text communication, people might read a message and assign a voice and physical characteristics to another person, within their own heads. Without visual cues, the mind can associate traits to another person according to their own needs and desires, which is a possibility on the phone.

Disassociative imagination – when people create an imaginary character online which exists in a different dimension. It becomes a game to play out a fantasy, online fiction becomes offline fact leading to escapism, potentially an issue on the phone.

Minimisation of status and authority – when the lack of hierarchy causes changes in interactions with others, a consideration for phone therapy.

It can be helpful to view disinhibited behaviour as different aspects of a person which are revealed in different situations. Suler says that the concept of disinhibition shouldn't be viewed as a true aspect of identity, that we shouldn't be misled into thinking that someone's disinhibited behaviour is more truly who they are. He states that the self does not exist separate from the environment in which it is expressed, and that disinhibition is

> a part or process within personality dynamics no less real or important than other parts or processes. This is why many psychoanalytic clinicians believe that working with defences and resistance – the inhibitors of the personality structure – is so crucial to the success of the therapy.
>
> (2004, p. 325)

How might you experience disinhibition from a client on the phone? Suler refers to two opposite dimensions to disinhibition. 'Benign disinhibition' allows people to reveal their fears, kindness and emotions and is 'an attempt to better understand and develop oneself, to resolve interpersonal and intrapsychic problems or explore new emotional and experiential dimensions to one's identity' (2004, p. 321).

A clear advantage to visual anonymity is that the lack of eye contact allows clients to talk more freely about difficult issues, those that are humiliating or embarrassing. The client doesn't have to risk any physical expression of their therapist's judgement, shock or fear. They don't have to bear the slightest flicker of disapproval across the therapist's face. An obvious subject is sex – ranging from disclosure of infidelity, sex addiction, sexual abuse and exploration of gender identity. Discrimination of every kind, domestic abuse, rape – historical or recent – can be easier for clients to disclose without being seen. Likewise, taboo issues resulting in disenfranchised grief after ending an affair or stigmatised heartaches involving nonconformity, such as the shame of being a woman living apart from children, my private practice clients. In my experience, invisibility combined with the intimacy of speaking directly into the ear makes the phone an effective therapeutic medium for deep expression, healing and exploration of any next steps beneficial to or necessary for the client beyond therapy.

By contrast, Suler names the other dimension of online disinhibition as 'toxic disinhibition', saying it 'may simply be a blind catharsis', which could be an expression of anger, rudeness or hatefulness.

Here are a few scenarios of when toxic disinhibition might come into play. A client might blame you, criticise you, get angry with you or make passive aggressive and sarcastic comments. Their words and tone might be forthright or blunt. A client might ask you particularly pointed, direct or personal questions. It might feel like they offload without restraint, not allowing you a word in edgeways. They might behave in surprisingly unselfconscious ways which could feel discourteous to you, such as emptying the dishwasher, driving their car, feeding the cat or eating their lunch during the session. Be aware, however, that some of the above are also contracting matters that are covered elsewhere.

How you view or decide to work with disinhibition will be guided by your theoretical orientation and therapy style. The following considerations might be helpful.

With visual privacy, clients can feel a change in power balance, what Suler calls a minimisation of status (2004, p. 324). Although therapists sometimes worry that therapy boundaries or they themselves will be challenged more easily, clients can benefit from a greater sense of control and expression when they receive phone therapy. In his paper, Suler suggests that if someone contains aggression when they are physically present but expresses aggression online, both behaviours reflect aspects of them which make them behave aggressively in certain situations and non-aggressively in others. The same would be true of someone who is shy in person and outgoing online. There will be times when this forms part of the work and exploration in supervision should support you with this.

A collaborative approach to the work, checking in on the relationship between you and how the medium of the phone is working for you both can create the opportunity for honest discussion about any disinhibited behaviour occurring for or between either of you.

Disinhibition might also lead a client to struggle with processing as the phone allows some clients to disclose deeper material earlier than when face to face. The BACP OPT competence framework (2021) states that we need 'an ability to help clients who may be disinhibited to pace their communications in a manner that makes it more likely that they are able to process material they are disclosing'. In addition, 'rapid disclosure of sensitive information and/or uninhibited expression of emotion that risks leaving the client vulnerable or overwhelmed'.

> *A client who had received a considerable amount of face to face therapy before working with me on the phone really noticed the difference. She would say, 'Wow, it's jaw dropping how much we've covered today'. Working collegially, we discussed her use of sessions and agreed that she would say when she felt she had reached her capacity to process material for the day. We would end sessions early, according to her processing ability. This has a very different feel to client avoidance which would be worked with by other means.*

Trust can be developed very quickly over the phone, sometimes even established after the first or second session. Invisibility or visual privacy can allow clients to express themselves and their emotions more freely than when face to face. This can be a liberating relief for clients, but some can feel vulnerable or overwhelmed at the end of a session.

> *At the beginning of her third session, a client told me that that after her previous session she felt icy cold and shaky, saying that it took resolve to phone*

me that day. She went on to explain that she normally represses emotions, describing herself as more of a thinker than a feeling person. I thanked her for telling me and gently assured her that we will check in during session to make sure that sessions progress at a pace that is manageable for her and allow time at the end to monitor pace and process.

I was struck by two things in relation to this client. I was greatly relieved that she told me how she had experienced the session, she could have simply ended the work perhaps without even telling me why. But without being seen or seeing me, the phone had allowed her to disclose feelings and strong somatic reaction this caused. We worked collaboratively together, keeping a virtual eye on any negative reactions to visual anonymity and ending well after about a year of phone therapy.

If you feel that a lot of early disclosure has taken place, you might decide to gently slow the session down, moderating the pace by lowering your tone, pausing and reflecting on the session. I'm usually transparent about this, 'you've shared a lot today, expressed a lot of emotion today, you might experience further feelings coming up after the session, that's ok, you might like to talk about how you felt at your next session'. Good grounding is important on the phone and more on this can be found in Chapter 8.

Setting and holding clear boundaries – start and finish times, privacy, payment terms, cancellation policy and what constitutes a Did Not Attend (DNA) – will give you a framework to lean on should a client express a disinhibited response when disagreements occur. As inhibitions can lower on the phone, some boundaries can be more difficult to manage which is why unambiguous contracting is essential. Without being able to see you, boundaries might also be pushed by curious clients asking questions about how you look, your age, whether you're in a relationship, where you're located and so on. Being clear about how much you're prepared to disclose in advance can help you hold boundaries if such questions are asked.

Therapist disinhibition

Let's start with many a therapist's worst scenario and anguished cry, 'I can't believe that I said that, I would never say anything like that if I was working face to face!' Perhaps, this is about being too direct or feeling triggered and saying something inappropriate. Sometimes, this happens when client and therapist's disinhibition collide. The starting point for managing therapist disinhibition is to know it occurs and keep our fingers on our pulse, particularly with clients we find challenging. Feeling triggered when working face to face is challenging too; at least one advantage to working on the phone is that the client can't see your face which allows you to discharge emotion by frowning, screwing up your face or biting your lip rather than verbalising it. Do your best to pause and take a breath.

It might be useful to say, 'Hmm, I'll need to think about this or what you said or what I feel about that'. Exercising restraint can be aided by checking the client's meaning, 'Correct me if I've not understood you but did you say', or, if you know you were blunt, 'Ah, let me reword that, it didn't come out quite the way I intended'. Take the matter to supervision and explore it fully to work through any rupture with the client. Just as importantly, use supervision to let go of any embarrassment, shame, regret, loss of confidence or feelings of being de-skilled.

Therapist disinhibition on the phone might not even be about what the client or therapist says. Bear in mind our heightened sense of hearing, particularly our reaction to sudden noise and our tendency to startle, has higher levels of arousal and irritation, particularly to human sounds such as a loud breathing, swallowing, chewing, sniffing, finger tapping or fidgeting by clients. Notice if you start to feel annoyed and consider whether noises need to be addressed to avoid an unhelpful, uninhibited knee-jerk response or whether you can adjust to them.

Although there can be concern about disinhibition causing therapists to be too directive, in my experience, it's not all negative. Working collaboratively, I tell clients that I will on occasion clarify that I have understood them, that I might butt in to do this and we will check in and communicate about how we are working which allows me, when I feel it will be helpful, to cut to the chase. This could be when there is a lot of story, detail or repetition. It is possible to do this without the client feeling undermined, perhaps by saying something like, 'I'm going to come in here and just check that I'm understanding you correctly'. Having reflected on my approach with a number of clients who have blended therapy, a combination of phone and face-to-face sessions, I notice I am able to be more directive on the phone which clients have found helpful.

Assumptions and unconscious bias

Making assumptions, jumping to conclusions about what might not be true for the client is a blind spot therapists work hard to avoid. The more we assume, the more we distance ourselves from the client's experience and their distress. We know that by not buying into assumptions we reduce the tendency to make judgements. Without seeing our client to clarify understanding, we need to be especially vigilant to distinguish between facts and assumptions.

You might receive limited information about a client before their first session, a brief outline of the presenting issue, their age or gender for example, but information like gender identity, race, disability, cultural or religious beliefs might not be available to you. You can't determine these facts from a client's tone, pitch, intonation or accent. Phone therapy requires us to work in an open way and ask more questions. I lean on the medium of the phone by telling the client that as I can't see them, I am likely to ask quite a few questions as it's important for me to fact check and verify my understanding. I believe that clients accept and appreciate that I'm making every effort to understand them. In addition, by explaining my need to on occasion ask more questions that I would do if we were physically present, I am at greater ease when asking what might appear obvious if I'm not sure.

Without visual cues, asking questions rather than assuming can make the work cleaner, less cluttered with what we take for granted when we are able to see a client. Supported by supervision, checking facts and understanding can facilitate empathy towards the client, a close working alliance and a clearer sense of projection and transference.

However, if an assumption is the basis of a judgement, how can you be non-judgemental if you're making assumptions you aren't even aware of? Unconscious bias, all the assumptions we unwittingly make due to the biases shaped in our upbringing and life experiences, requires that we examine our unconscious conditioning and work with personal awareness. Not making assumptions, listening well and holding back from asking questions that are more to do with our learning and awareness than knowing enough to ensure you are understanding the client's frame of reference are crucial. Unconscious bias is considered further in Chapter 7.

References

Aeschlimann, M., Knebel, J. F., Murray, M. M., & Clarke, S. (2008). Emotional pre-eminence of human vocalizations. *Brain Topography*, *20*(4), 239–248. https://doi.org/10.1007/s10548-008-0051-8

Allen, S. (1990). The rise of New Zealand intonation. In A. Bell & J. Holmes (Eds.), *New Zealand ways of speaking English* (pp. 115–128). Multilingual Matters.

Antonioni, D. T. (1973). *A field study comparison of counselor empathy, concreteness and client self-exploration in face-to-face and telephone counseling during first and second interviews*. Doctoral Thesis, University of Wisconsin.

BACP. (2021). *Online and phone therapy competence framework*. www.bacp.co.uk/media/10849/bacp-online-and-phone-therapy-competence-framework-feb21.pdf

Bedi, R. P. (2006). Concept mapping the client's perspective on counseling alliance formation. *Journal of Counseling Psychology*, *53*(1), 26–35. https://doi.org/10.1037/0022-0167.53.1.26

Bedi, R. P., & Duff, C. T. (2014). Client as expert: A Delphi poll of clients' subjective experience of therapeutic alliance formation variables. *Counselling Psychology Quarterly*, *27*(1), 1–18. https://doi.org/10.1080/09515070.2013.857295

Cameron, D. (2003). Gender issues in language change. *Annual Review of Applied Linguistics*, *23*, 187–201. https://doi.org/10.1017/s0267190503000266

Christogiorgos, S., Vassilopoulou, V., Florou, A., Xydou, V., Douvou, M., Vgenopoulou, S., & Tsiantis, J. (2010). Telephone counselling with adolescents and countertransference phenomena: Particularities and challenges. *British Journal of Guidance & Counselling*, *38*(3), 313–325. https://doi.org/10.1080/03069885.2010.482394

Day, S. X., & Schneider, P. L. (2002). Psychotherapy using distance technology: A comparison of face-to-face, video, and audio treatment. *Journal of Counseling Psychology*, *49*(4), 499–503. https://doi.org/10.1037/0022-0167.49.4.499

Drummond, R. (2014, August 19). 10 theories on how uptalk originated. *BBC News*. www.bbc.co.uk/news/magazine-28785865

Guy, G., Horvath, B., Vonwiller, J., Daisley, E., & Rogers, I. (1986). An intonational change in progress in Australian English. *Language in Society*, *15*(1), 23–51. https://doi.org/10.1017/s0047404500011635

Horowitz, S. (2012). *The universal sense: How hearing shapes the mind*. Bloomsbury.

Klofstad, C. A. (2016). Candidate voice pitch influences election outcomes. *Political Psychology*, *37*(5), 725–738. https://doi.org/10.1111/pops.12280

Macaulay, R. (2007). The social art: Language and its uses (second edition). Oxford: Oxford University Press, 2006. xii + 244 pp. £11.99. ISBN 0-19-518796-2. *Forum for Modern Language Studies*, *43*(1), 104. https://doi.org/10.1093/fmls/cql154

Matthews, P. H. (2014). *The Concise Oxford Dictionary of linguistics*. Oxford University Press.

Reeves, N. (2015). The use of telephone and Skype in psychotherapy: Reflections of an attachment therapist. In L. Cundy (Ed.), *Love in the age of the internet* (pp. 125–152). Taylor & Francis.

Rogers, C. R. (1975). Empathic: An unappreciated way of being. *The Counseling Psychologist*, *5*(2), 2–10. https://doi.org/10.1177/001100007500500202

Rosenfield, M. (1997). *Counselling by telephone (professional skills for counsellors series)* (1st ed.). SAGE.

Sanders, P. (2007). *Using counselling skills on the telephone* (3rd ed.). PCCS.

Suler, J. (2004). The online disinhibition effect. *Cyber Psychology & Behavior*, *7*(3), 321–326. https://doi.org/10.1089/1094931041291295

Trager, G. L. (1958). Paralanguage: A first approximation. *Studies in Linguistics*, *13*, 1–12.

Warren, P. (2005). Patterns of late rising in New Zealand English: Intonational variation or intonational change? *Language Variation and Change*, *17*(2). https://doi.org/10.1017/s095439450505009x

Chapter 4

Theoretical modalities used in phone therapy

Phone or indeed any digital therapy is not a model in itself. The BACP (2021) does not deem any one modality to be more effective than another, and the UK Council for Psychotherapy (UKCP) (2021) encourages members to think through modality-related issues that may arise from a particular way of working.

Maxine Rosenfield (1997, p. 67) asserts that 'telephone counselling and telephone psychotherapy have aspects of practice which do not fit neatly into any single orientation used for face to face work'. Her view is that humanistic orientations and cognitive behavioural therapy, 'where client encouraged to become aware of and control aspects of behaviour – seem more adaptable than psychoanalytic orientations'. She encourages psychodynamic therapists to consider how they will adapt their way of working on the phone, pointing out that a classically trained psychoanalytic therapist who 'is silent except when making an interpretation is not likely to be very successful of the telephone, when clients often require encouragement and verbal gestures'. However, she does state 'On the other hand, it could be argued that the telephone could enhance transference and for that reason it might be a very useful medium'. During the COVID-19 pandemic, psychoanalytic therapist Murdin (2021), who transitioned her practice to the phone, deliberates this and wider considerations for analytic therapy by comparing the value of the therapeutic couch to the value of the telephone.

The COVID-19 pandemic will, I hope, have encouraged new discussion of the use and value of phone therapy across different theoretical models. To explore the adaptation of different modalities for use on the phone, I asked therapists from a number of theoretical approaches to share their experience.

Person-centred

Joanna Farmer is a person-centred therapist who has a private practice which includes providing staff counselling. She teaches person-centred counselling on an integrative counselling diploma-level course at South Gloucestershire and Stroud College.

Most of the phone therapy I provide is short-term counselling to members working for a large union. When I started, I wondered whether it was possible

DOI: 10.4324/9781003253396-4

to offer a person-centred approach in this role and imagined that I would have to work integratively. What surprised me is how powerful short-term person-centred phone therapy can be.

I have found that the six necessary and sufficient conditions work well on the phone.

Psychological contact, which some might imagine would be weakened without visuals, is often more immediate and intimate than working face to face. When I train student counsellors, they ask how this is possible as person-centred work takes time. In my experience, by the end of the first session if the client has felt heard, valued, understood and trusted to be themselves, something internal can shift slightly, and they can build on that in short-term therapy. On the phone, the relationship has a different quality to it which really aids the work, and this quality comes from the intimacy of the medium.

When clients invite me into their world, I often have an image of opening and entering the back of the wardrobe to their own private Narnia. I've never been there before, and they don't know a lot of what is there. On the phone, this happens very quickly and at the end of the call I feel like I am emerging from somewhere. Not being in a room together, we are suspended in time and space in their world, which feels more intimate, real and immediate. Rather than meaning that there is less available when working with only one sense, I find I hear the important things, the subtle meanings which are right on the edge of the client's awareness. The throw-away comments, the words they use, tone of their voice, all those paralinguistic communications mean I am really close to the client's personal internal world so that empathy feels even more possible. Empathy is a very active process, if it was passive, you wouldn't be able to sustain it and stay engaged on the phone for 50 minutes. I have found that I work more with the delicate process of empathy on the phone.

I experience the client's disinhibition, the things they might not say in the room as congruence. I feel that it is better to explore how the experience was for the client rather than have a valued judgement of disinhibition. If you can work with immediacy and stay connected to what it might be like to have said it, particularly if there is a throw-away comment like, 'I can't believe I just said that' or a sense they said more than they thought they might, it can release the client. In my experience, almost without exception, although it might be uncomfortable for example feelings of shame, you can work with it and there is something that feels like a relief or an openness that clients value.

My congruence on the phone feels different. I notice that when I meet a client for the first time face to face, I am very much the counsellor. I am thinking about the room, the chair, the client entering my space and I feel a bit inhibited. As there is less sense of being seen in the role of counsellor, I am completely comfortable meeting the client on the phone for the first time, so I am more congruent. This kick-starts the work as there is that immediate connection, clients let down their safety screens and don't block out vulnerable parts. They can really benefit from not being looked at, observed in the chair.

The therapy room is a container for the client and the work, and without it, I have to be more of a container. The power dynamics are exacerbated by being in the therapy room, and on the phone, I am released. I have a more solid sense of personal power without the solid walls. I am ethical and this is in me, not defined by the walls of the counselling room. I enjoy that there aren't these external indicators that say I'm trustworthy. I know I am, and I communicate that because I am at ease with myself. In person-centred work, if I can trust myself, I am more likely to trust the client and they are more likely to trust themself. I think that is why person-centred work on the phone can move quickly, we are not navigating the roles in the same way.

I notice that I am a lot more proactive at the beginning of the work, inviting the client in and making my presence known. I wouldn't hold a silence of any length at the beginning of the work, and I will check in with the client more, 'I wonder where you are?', to explore where they've been internally, during that pause. Because I can't see the client, I can assume that as we are both in this process, we are sharing something, yet so often, they haven't been there as it has triggered another thought that they haven't said out aloud yet.

To me, person-centred work is a spiritual practice in which you are encountering another human being, accepting their very essence, working with who and how they are in the world and in relationship without judgement. I feel that on the phone, unconditional positive regard is even more possible. One of the most exciting things about working on the phone is the disembodied voice. I'm not trying to manage my feelings about how they look or any other physical aspect of their being I might have momentary positive and negative judgements about.

There can be an assumption that it takes a long time to weaken conditions of worth. In my experience they can begin to weaken in one session and afterwards, a client can say to their partner, 'Don't speak to me like that'. That is the beginning of a weakening of a condition of worth that they are not worth anything and that they can be spoken to in a derogatory way. Having feelings honoured can shift something. The change process of person-centred work, the client becoming more congruent and the weakening of conditions of worth can happen on the phone even during short-term counselling.

I worked with a client who had been signed off of work after a false accusation. He was so angry he didn't feel it was safe to be around his family, so he had taken himself off to his bedroom and they were leaving food outside the door. If this was counselling in person, it would have been the equivalent of going to his house and sitting on the end of his bed. Being with such a client was so intimate and powerful. He would never have accessed face-to-face therapy, but by the end of the work, in just six sessions, he came out of the room and back into the family home.

A persistent theme in my work is clients feeling disempowered and bullied. Starting counselling with their back in the corner, by the end of six sessions, many say they have a voice. They have been listened to with such respect and trust from me and because I don't try to change the client or think they should be different, they learn to trust their own voice and are less likely to be bullied. Clients might start saying they are going to leave the profession and end by saying they will leave the job because they know the problem is not them as an individual. They feel more empowered and that's the heart of person-centred therapy.

Person-centred therapy should not be dismissed as just a listening ear or that you can't do much using this modality over the phone. My experience is that profound work can happen quite quickly, and the phone can enhance it.

Psychodynamic

Donna Stratton is a psychodynamic therapist who has a private practice, works with young people and adults within a charity and is a psychodynamic counselling course tutor at The Counselling Foundation in Bedford.

All of my core training is psychodynamic. When the COVID-19 pandemic occurred, I had additional training on working remotely and discovered that phone therapy involved using a familiar object but in a different way. Even though you have a phone in your hand every day, it's a mistake to think you can just jump into phone therapy. It is the same but different, so my advice would be to think about it, plan it, check it and get further training.

I still use all of the core psychodynamic basic skills and fundamentals. On the phone, the therapeutic alliance develops in the same way, and it surprised me how quickly this can happen. I found you can still create a safe place for the client in their own environment rather than the therapy room. I start the session by checking that the client is settled and comfortable in a private place, whether it is in their house or their car, the rituals around attending the sessions. I make the client aware of practicalities like session times showing up on their phone bill and about counselling and how I work. This gives them time to settle during their first session.

The assessment is much the same as face to face. I have a robust system in place and ask questions about previous illnesses, medication, self-harm, suicidal thoughts and drug and alcohol use. I check for risk, you need to be very clear about who you are talking to, what their issues are and what they are wanting from therapy. I have found my own style for asking these questions on the phone, and I might be a bit more cautious with some clients, as I don't have sight of the person.

At the beginning of the work, I am a little more chatty, encouraging the client to engage with me to get the rhythm of talking going between us. Once this is established, I retreat a bit and let them fill the gaps as they become more confident. This is different to the psychodynamic harshness that people might view my modality as having. I want the client to come back and being too analytic might cause clients to run off into the hills. Without body language, I adjust to being a bit warmer and friendly initially, until the client gets into the flow.

There is stillness and calmness in the therapy room. I was disconcerted at first by how much clients were distracted on the phone, walking around their kitchen and making a cup of tea. I learnt to set out the frame at the beginning about what

I would expect during a session, then reminding them, to keep them focused on valuing their session time. Perhaps, a humanistic therapist would be of the view that the client is having a drink because they need a drink, whereas a psychodynamic therapist would think they should be dedicating their time to their therapy and start to interpret this. Freud said that sometimes a cigar is just a cigar but there are times, especially if they are regularly distracted that I will bring it into the work.

There are a number of psychological elements to think through which work just as well, for example Freud's structural model or the positions from Klein. Without visuals, I find Bion's concept of reverie important, being in that daydream state, trying to think about being that containing mind in a more intense way on the phone. When you are role modelling thinking for the client, it can be hard to interject, you need to verbalise it a bit more. They can't see you trying to find your words, so I might tell them 'I want to say something but let me just think about that for a moment'. I prefix things more, I might say I am imagining something before spending time thinking about it with the client. On the phone, I am imagining and wondering with the client more. In the room there is a quietness, a harshness where I would hold back and let them think about it more. On the phone I'm more inviting, to encourage the client to talk to me. I am more active and engaging on the phone, not just sitting back as I might do in the room.

Personally, I think this adjustment is necessary for psychodynamic phone therapy, but you need to keep yourself in check. On occasion I've pushed the boundary out a little bit. You've got to be mindful not to overstep the mark and find yourself being unprofessional or acting out or finishing the punch line to a client's joke. We are human and if you are a little out of boundary it can be tempting to slide the boundary further. After the initial stages, you have to pull the boundary back. The work can be quite tiring until you find your feet with it.

I listen to the client's pace, talking quickly might mean they are in crisis. Sometimes, clients are chatty, and material can tumble out of them quite quickly. If they are quieter, I use my voice to draw them in. It's amazing how intimate the phone is. You can hear people breathing and get to know people well enough to know if they are smiling or crying or thinking. Silences can be hard to judge when you first start working on the phone. Does the client like silence or do they find it punishing? I use silences a lot, but I keep silences shorter on the phone and I might talk about it more than in the room. If I feel they can handle it, I'll leave longer silences. Talking over clients happens and I set the rules about how this operates by saying, 'If I talk over you I will stop and let you carry on, so we can avoid the need to apologise'.

Transference on the phone occurs much in the same way as it does in the room as the client narrates their story. When they start acting it out, especially with you, there is a real opportunity to explore Malan's triangle of Person in the here and now on the phone, 'This is what I'm hearing and it reminds me of what your mother said to you'. I don't feel that changes much. I might do more questioning and clarifying, but I might not go as all in on the phone. It is still about the client doing the work and me being the mirror at that point rather than the blank screen.

I find that countertransference occurs quicker on the phone because my mind wanders more, and I feel freer by not being locked into the visual of the person. It might be their tone of voice that I hear more acutely which stirs me more quickly, but I still deal with it the same way as I would in the room – thinking about it, talking about it and taking it to supervision as appropriate.

All client defences are alive and active, they are there for a reason, their coping mechanism. Sometimes, they are a bit more prominent or obvious on the phone and they can become quite a big part of the work, but I work with them in the same way as in the room.

Before the COVID-19 pandemic, my modality and way of working would not have been something clients would have been able to access on the phone easily. I feel really positive about including a wider group of people now that we are being more open-minded about phone work. So many clients have said to me 'I couldn't have told you half of the things I have if I had to sit in a room and face you'. Not having to sit in a room with you feeling shame and embarrassment has really enabled access to clients who probably wouldn't have come for therapy if the room was the only option.

Also, it gives a softer, more human approach to psychodynamic therapy. Before now, if a client couldn't get to the room, there would be no session. If they relocated, we would have to stop; but now we have the ability to think more broadly beyond a forced ending that can feel quite punishing and cruel sometimes. A bit of consistency and continuity while they settle into a new job or home can be beneficial for clients. We can still be working to an ending if there is a referral elsewhere, but it doesn't have to be our ending on top of all the other endings. It does feel kinder now that it doesn't have to be so regimented. We still have our fundamentals and core skills, but we can be blended in what we do and decide on what is right for the client using a wider set of parameters.

Integrative transpersonal

Linda Gaskell is an Integrative Transpersonal psychotherapist who works with young people and adults within a charity and in private practice.

I find that there are similarities in working on the phone to working face to face. My approach is relational, building a containing relationship with my clients so they feel safe to do the work. The transpersonal approach is about a deep listening to my client's distress and how they articulate this, how the soul might speak, and this often comes in the form of the imaginal through metaphor, archetypal stirrings which present through a myth or fairy tale or in the silences, tears or bodily responses, the wounded parts of my clients.

On the phone, I might share a bit more to encourage a dialogue. I might say, 'I'm sensing . . . I'm feeling' and invite the client to step in and start to contribute. This is a bit different to when I work face to face where I observe the body language and I might hold my own personal insights a bit more. On the phone I check in more to track my clients, noticing the silences, their breath or sighs. I use somatic responses, what I sense in my body and what my clients describe is happening in their body, as I find it's a helpful way to attune myself to my clients and what is happening to them when on the phone. For example if I am aware that I'm clenching my hands or jaw, I will share this with my client and say, 'I'm wondering how you are?', and we might play with that, I might ask them to amplify the clenched fist which allows them to engage with the feelings that may be stirred such as anger.

I appreciate the space for reverie on the phone, it's a bit like the psychoanalytic couch, allowing the client to daydream and ponder. Maybe they would in the room, face to face, but because they are not seen, they are much more unguarded and allows them to be free with their thoughts and feelings. I find it allows me space to rest rather than being vigilant that can happen in face to face or on zoom. In the resting is a deep listening, I wait for something to be said that needs to be looked at, that breaks though the story and captures my attention. It might come through my bodily feelings or a breath, tears or imaginal offerings. The attending to these murmurings, often subtle and nuanced, is where the soul work lies.

I work with transference and countertransference. I listen with sensitivity to what is activated within myself. This is very important on the phone, the unconscious material that my client is not aware of that I may be holding and attending too in my own body. I listen deeply to what is being stirred within myself, the felt experience, which informs me about what is going on within my client's world. I am aware of what role I might be holding in the transference, just like when working face to face. This might be information that I hold on to and helps to inform our work together.

On the phone I might reveal more, offering an image of what has been stirred. For example, my sense of something 'volcanic' which will allow the client to agree or say, 'No, it doesn't feel like that, it feels more like this'. I offer more of what my process is on the phone, I hold it in a different way than when I work face to face. I check in more, particularly around challenge by saying, 'I wonder how that was for you to hear me say that or ask that?' I do lots of checking out in different ways, as without seeing the client's body language it is a bit harder to gauge the impact of what is said.

I work somatically with trauma which is still possible on the phone. I've found that some clients can explore a bodily reaction without feeling as self-conscious on the phone. If the client feels there is a need for flight, to run, perhaps feeling cornered, working on the phone allows them uninhibited space for movement. As I am not watching them, they might use their body in a way that is loosening, just like an animal shaking off the attack, releasing the traumatic event. Not being seen, there is permission for this, and we can talk it through together and imagine them responding from a place of agency rather than collapse and fear, which can be deeply healing for a client.

The phone works well for hypervigilant clients and younger clients who feel safer with the privacy of their own room. I find that for young people particularly, the phone allows them to express themselves more freely and fits in with their life around school.

An example is a young client I worked with who suffered from social anxiety, especially around going into school. Each week, step by step, on the phone I walked beside her as she visualised arriving at school. I would ask, 'Where are we now?' and she described how she imagined entering the school gate. On the phone, listening to each other, I was able to encourage her to check in with her reality, which when anxious, would often have a distorted lens, believing everyone is looking at and judging her. She was able to describe entering the classroom and I could ask, 'What is it like to look around?' She replied that the other students looked at her for a few seconds and I said, 'What's that like, that they looked at you and then got on with their day?' she replied that it is ok, a relief. Through the imaginal, we were collaboratively able to be alongside each other, walking from home to school to classroom, which was very powerful for this client. I had my vision of it, she had hers, but we were attuned, going through the same experience together. In her bedroom she was able to have an embodied experience of moving around, feeling it was ok. Her body wasn't reacting in a hypervigilant way. She was able to feel that it is ok, that she is ok, in an embodied and memory-making way. I don't know if we would have had the same experience if we were to have worked with each other face to face.

As a transpersonal therapist, part of the modality I trained in was psychosynthesis, which includes working with subpersonalities and the process of integration, as you build a relationship with the different sub parts of the psyche. I find that on the phone, working with different subpersonalities is a good way to understand the client. For example recently when exploring with a client who has an eating disorder, we worked with an aspect of the client which is a perfectionist, who is controlling along with a more vulnerable, younger part of my client who is starved of attention. On the phone I'm able to encourage this a bit more by asking 'How would this part look to you, how would they come alive for you?' and we start to get a mutual visual that we can work with together and how these different parts interact with each other, such as being bullied and overlooked and with time, the work is in finding a more compassionate balanced voice.

I found during COVID-19 restrictions that phone sessions were very holding for my clients. Some clients chose to remain on the phone for various reasons. For some, if our work started on the phone, it was where our relationship was built, and it felt more comfortable to stay on the phone whilst others choose to stay on the phone due to changes in their circumstances such as having a new baby.

Now, I offer my clients blended therapy, a combination of face to face and phone. For example if they can't make the session, we can now have it on the phone rather than completely missing the session. It is curious, which clients will flourish working remotely and which prefer blended. This experience varies from client to client. One client who started working with me face to face and then moved to the phone initially commented, 'This is weird', but after this the client settled and enjoyed being on the phone, describing the experience as more intimate. She was more open to talk about things that in the room she may have been more guarded about. However, some clients were desperate to return to meeting face to face, especially those clients impacted by the isolation of lockdowns.

Pluralistic

Michelle Nicholson is a pluralistic counsellor who is employed by a university and founded Hyperemesis Counselling, a specialist service for women affected by severe pregnancy sickness.

My core training 20 years ago was in person-centred counselling, but since then I have drawn on motivational interviewing, solution-focused techniques and writing therapy in my work where appropriate. Phone counselling fits naturally with the pluralistic approach because pluralism recognises that each client has their own unique needs and preferences, and one size doesn't fit all.

The main advantages of phone therapy are that it allows clients to access counselling in circumstances where this wouldn't otherwise be possible or where sessions by video are not wanted. For five years, I was the only therapist offering specialist hyperemesis gravidarum (HG) counselling in the UK. Since many clients were isolated and unable to leave their homes or beds due to pregnancy sickness symptoms, phone therapy worked particularly well. Many clients felt uncomfortable being seen due to the degree of their physical debilitation leaving them unable to shower or manage housework often for several weeks or months. Some needed to lie down or break off from the session to vomit. Arrangements for this were discussed during the first session, including an agreed word to let me know they were ending the call, with a view to phoning me back within their session time if needed.

I frequently encouraged clients to cognitively reframe their negative thinking. Women living with HG often struggle to cope with a sense of frustration around their pregnancy not being as they had anticipated. Some might for example describe self-critical thoughts about their incapacity to eat healthily, engage with their pregnancy or cope as well as women without HG. Counselling enabled women to reframe this and practise more helpful mind-sets around 'good enough pregnancy' or being part of a worldwide community of HG survivors. All of this was possible by telephone, while honouring each client's need to remain comfortable at home.

Often, I was able to gauge a client's HG symptoms by how they sounded on the phone. Their tone of voice told me much about how unwell they were or whether they were lying down because they were too ill to sit up, and this was useful in deciding how to work in ways that were most suitable for them.

The university students I work with are often surprised by how effective phone sessions are, particularly, if they have moved from online video to telephone due to technical difficulties. Like my HG clients, they sometimes hold fantasies of what they believe university life should look like and reframing with more helpful mind-sets can be useful. It can be quite challenging but also transformational. When I work by phone, I also email clients links or signposts to other resources, available within and outside of the university.

I have noticed that when a client is very distressed, unwell, or suicidal, I sometimes find myself almost hugging the phone, holding it as if I'm demonstrating empathy, cradling it, leaning forward even though they can't see me. It's not conscious. I am so focused on the client and what is going on for them and I am sure they pick up on this in my voice.

I tend to ask clients more questions on the phone including details of any disability or medical condition that it would be useful for me to know about. This is particularly important when I work with students at risk of drug and alcohol addiction or an eating disorder. For example working face to face, heavy alcohol use might be smelt or reduced body weight seen, so without visual cues on the phone, I ask more in-depth questions and generally find this a manageable way of working.

Working by telephone has an obvious practical advantage for students who live and work on a large campus or are temporarily based abroad. Since students tend to use mobile phones, discussing and contracting for privacy is important right from the beginning. At the end of sessions, I encourage them to manage transition time, allowing space before rushing out to meet someone or returning to essay writing straight away. Clients are emailed guidelines in advance, but I do occasionally have to help them set boundaries around privacy if they have accepted a call in a public place. It happens in private practice too. Working internationally, a client once called me while she was in a supermarket saying it didn't matter as no one there understood English. We ended the call and I waited for her to go home, unpack shopping and phone me back from a private space. Maybe this is more likely to occur with younger generations who are normalised to have conversations anywhere. In my day, I could have spoken to someone only if the phone was plugged into a wall. For one of my ongoing HG clients, living in a country that was hit by a severe hurricane, working by phone enabled us to continue with sessions while her online service of email and video had been lost. I hadn't been sure that her phone reception would work in these circumstances, and it was such a relief when she phoned me at her scheduled time, allowing her to attend the session.

Often, I suggest to other therapists, particularly pluralistic counsellors, that they might be surprised by how effective phone therapy can be and how much clients appreciate it. Before setting up a specialist private practice that provided sessions by telephone only due to the nature of the clients' specific medical condition (HG), counselling by phone had not been my preferred way of working, or even something I had thought much about. Since working in this way, I have really come to appreciate the value and benefits of phone therapy and what it offers to clients. As an experienced counsellor, telephone therapy is an approach that has been easily incorporated into my practice upon completion of relevant CPD training and one that could be adopted by any therapist once they have gained sufficient knowledge, skills, confidence and supervisory support.

I'm proud of the phone counselling I provide. Knowing how much clients benefit from it, I appreciate the value of the phone in terms of what it offers.

Cognitive behavioural therapy

There is a large body of research that shows that phone-delivered CBT is success-ful, and Irvine et al. (2020, p. 130) state that

> Some scholars (e.g. Lingley-Pottie and McGrath, 2007; Turner et al., 2018; Webb, 2014) point to the possibility that in telephone-delivered therapy there may be an alternative type of alliance at work, one that is qualitatively differ-ent to that which is established face-to-face but is nonetheless facilitative of therapeutic work.

Rosenfield (1997, p. 63) states that cognitive behavioural therapies 'can work well on the telephone because they require the client to be an active participant, empowered by the process of the work and the counsellor-client partnership'. A study by Hammond (2012) using data from 39,000 patients in seven Improving Access to Psychological Therapies (IAPT) services in the East of England were used to compare CBT delivered face to face versus over the phone, revealed that cognitive therapy over the phone was just as effective as meeting in person. Con-venience and cost-effectiveness were cited as clear advantages not only in the UK.

> In a global context the potential is enormous for spreading access to effective psychological therapies to the millions of people affected by depression and anxiety. As the availability of mobile phone technology in low- and middle-income countries grows, people now have the potential of having a therapist in their pocket, transcending traditional barriers to the receipt of effective treatments.
>
> (Hammond, 2012)

With CBT's emphasis on task and without being physically present, being mindful of a warm tone and welcome use of encouragers, pacing, checking understanding and all the communication and core skills covered in Chapter 3 are particularly important. Without visual cues consideration to the format of sessions is advisable to ensure strategically timed use of questionnaires and outcome measures, so too will be the verbal adaptation of diagrams and models for use on the phone.

CBT therapists might find Irvine and Drew's (2020) paper with practical sug-gestions for Psychological Wellbeing Practitioners (PWPs) working within IAPT useful. This resource gleaned from two years of phone delivery of low-intensity IAPT, as part of a larger project led by the University of Manchester, examined over 120 recorded telephone sessions including assessments, first and second treatment sessions. Their recommendations include:

- Take time to ask the client to briefly share how they have been or why they have accessed the service. Contrary to practitioner's concern that this will take up too much time, their research showed this not to be the case. Taking time puts the patient first and allows for further questioning and personalised conversations.

- Be responsive in the moment to a patient's disclosure. A short, compassionate response helps the patient to feel understood and acknowledged (all of the core skills in Chapter 3 are appropriate for CBT).
- Let the patient know how long the session is but avoid talking about having an agenda or meeting the systems requirements.
- Breakdown any long psychoeducational explanations into shorter sections (without visual aids, consider how the client will process information, see Chapter 8 for suggestions).
- Take time to talk through homework, clearly explaining the task and its benefits.
- Take particular care to verbally encourage patients, compliment achievements and motivate them to attend the next session.

Although it hasn't been possible to explore all modalities in this chapter, I hope the insights shared will encourage conversation between peers, tutors and supervisors about the adaptation of most, if not all, theoretical orientations for phone therapy.

References

BACP. (2021). *Online and phone therapy competence framework.* www.bacp.co.uk/media/10849/bacp-online-and-phone-therapy-competence-framework-feb21.pdf

Hammond, G. C. (2012, September 28). Comparative effectiveness of cognitive therapies delivered face-to-face or over the telephone: An observational study using propensity methods. *PLoS ONE.* https://journals.plos.org/plosone/article?id=10.1371/journal.pone.0042916

Irvine, A., & Drew, P. (2020, April). Telephone delivery of the NHS's IAPT service providing low-intensity psychological treatment for anxiety and depression disorders. *ResearchGate.* from www.researchgate.net/publication/340788591_Telephone_delivery_of_the_NHS's_IAPT_service_providing_low-intensity_psychological_treatment_for_anxiety_and_depression_disorders

Irvine, A., Drew, P., Bower, P., Brooks, H., Gellatly, J., Armitage, C. J., Barkham, M., McMillan, D., & Bee, P. (2020). Are there interactional differences between telephone and face-to-face psychological therapy? A systematic review of comparative studies. *Journal of Affective Disorders, 265,* 120–131. https://doi.org/10.1016/j.jad.2020.01.057

Lingley-Pottie, P., & McGrath, P. J. (2007, October). Distance therapeutic alliance. *Advances in Nursing Science, 30*(4), 353–366. https://doi.org/10.1097/01.ans.0000300184.94595.25

Murdin, L. (2021). Is anyone there? Use of the telephone and use of the couch. *British Journal of Psychotherapy, 37*(2), 234–243. https://doi.org/10.1111/bjp.12629

Rosenfield, M. (1997). *Counselling by telephone (professional skills for counsellors series)* (1st ed.). SAGE.

Turner, J., Brown, J. C., & Carpenter, D. T. (2018, January 30). Telephone-based CBT and the therapeutic relationship: The views and experiences of IAPT practitioners in a low-intensity service. *Journal of Psychiatric and Mental Health Nursing, 25*(5–6), 285–296. https://doi.org/10.1111/jpm.12440

UK Council for Psychotherapy (UKCP). (2021). *UKCP Guidelines for working online/ remotely.* from www.psychotherapy.org.uk/media/jrohoner/ukcp-guidelines-for-working-online-or-remotely-v1-0.pdf

Webb, C. (2014). *A qualitative study of the therapeutic alliance during telephone cognitive behavioural therapy: Clinicians' perspectives.* Doctoral Thesis, University of East Anglia, UK.

Chapter 5

The contract – working legally, professionally and ethically on the phone

When therapists work face to face with clients, they take responsibility for and have control over the physical space in which therapy takes place. Ethical phone therapy means that we consider how we will communicate securely at a distance and how we will advise and support our client's security too. A carefully thought through contracting process, procedures and boundaries related to remote therapy generally and phone therapy specifically needs to be clearly communicated and agreed with clients. Working legally, professionally and ethically is also about understanding that working from two different locations can be a fluctuating process as we adapt to shifting circumstances, such as glitches in technology and changing physical spaces of some clients.

Security and confidentiality relating to phones

Smartphones, mobile phones and landlines

Making clients aware of safety issues when they receive phone therapy includes knowing the risks related to the type of equipment they use. Although many people use smartphones, some might still use a landline or a basic mobile for which online security will not be of concern.

Even though we often call a smartphone a mobile phone, technically, the two terms refer to different devices. Both mobile phone and smartphone are mobile devices from which you can call and send texts, but only a smartphone has internet access. You won't be able to tell if a client calls you from a smartphone or a mobile phone from their phone number. Even if a client calls from a smartphone, they will be using the same technology as a client calling from a basic mobile phone or a landline. If the phone signal is poor, smartphone users are able to switch to Wi-Fi but only if they have activated Wi-Fi calling on their phone as this is not an automatic process. This means that equipment security considerations for phone therapy sometimes, but not always, include issues related to online therapy.

DOI: 10.4324/9781003253396-5

When is online security relevant for phone therapy?

If you or your client uses a smartphone with activated Wi-Fi calling when reception is poor, or indeed an online videoconference platform without video or a VoIP call, online security should be assessed and discussed with clients. Advancements in technology develop rapidly, but for now, key areas typically include:

Password protection – choosing strong or complex passwords are recommended, such as using three random words or the use of a growing number of phone fingerprint scanners.

Security updates – all manufacturers release regular updates that contain critical security updates; to keep devices protected they should be set to automatically update, where possible.

Public hotspots – the simplest precaution is not to connect to the internet using unknown hotspots and call instead from the mobile network, which will have built-in security. Avoid other sensitive transactions too, such as online banking using public Wi-Fi.

Whatever phone or device is used by you and your clients, more general online security should also be borne in mind. As technology advances and different types of devices are developed, so does their use by the therapeutic community. Appointments are arranged online (or by text), electronic calendars are scheduled, session notes are stored online and invoices and payments are generated electronically. It's very likely you will be sending emails, perhaps with an attached contract or to collect data such as outcome measures or questionnaires. Counselling services and individual practitioners will need to consider both security and accessibility when it comes to contracting, assessment and monitoring for remote working. Fortunately, home Wi-Fi in the UK is usually encrypted and provides automatic security and firewall updates. Other confidentiality considerations are shared laptops or home computers which might mean a client's privacy could be at stake without individual passwords. More on confidentiality and privacy is covered a little later in this chapter.

As a method of receiving payment for therapy, online banking is considered secure as long as security measures are taken. For example it is safer if multiple passwords are used for different accounts and changed regularly, anti-virus software should be updated regularly, and it is sensible to avoid public Wi-Fi for transactions unless a virtual private network (VPN) hides the IP address. For some, being careful about what is posted on social media is also a consideration, if information shared is the same or linked to what they use to answer banking security questions, perhaps a child's birthday or a pet's name.

A good place to find out more about online security is the National Cyber Security Centre www.ncsc.gov.uk and the UK government's website Cyber aware www.ncsc.gov.uk/cyberaware/home.

Therapist's digital footprint

The BACP Online and Phone Therapy (OPT) competence framework (2021) draws our attention to our own digital footprint and the BACP recommends that 'practitioners maintain a clear distinction between their personal and professional online presence'.

Most professional bodies, including the BACP, UKCP and BPS, provide guidance to practitioners on managing social media. Psychotherapist Aaron Balick (2017) writes about the benefits of having a digital policy to provide clarity around terms of engagement with clients. His motivation for the policy was linked to the impact of a client Googling and reading information about him while she was in a distressed state. Fortunately, he and his client were able to work through the experience which he describes in his paper 'TMI in the Transference LOL: psychoanalytic reflections on Google, Social Networking and Digital Impingement'. Balick is generous in allowing therapists to view and adapt his digital policy which can be found on his website www.aaronbalick.com.

Main security issues in the provision of phone therapy

Risk of eavesdropping

Privacy is crucial and is a key element of discussion when I contract with clients. More can be found on this in the next chapter.

Phone hacking

Landlines, mobile phones, and VoIP systems are all at risk of being hacked, listened in on and compromised; however, phone calls, text messages and voice messages are more secure than any other telecommunication system. If you communicate via messaging, sending a text message is more secure than a message sent via Wi-Fi.

Voice assistant activation

Avoid unintentional actions and voice recording by turning listening devices such as Alexa and Siri off during a session. In addition to the risk of hacking, leaving your data and privacy at risk, the response from a voice assistant misinterpreting you and being activated by a mistaken 'wake word' will be a sudden, alarming breach of privacy and disruption to the session.

My own experience of being shocked into awareness of voice assistant activation was during a face-to-face session when a client inadvertently activated a 'wake word' on my smartphone. My phone was in a cupboard, and I had turned off my ring and notification volume before the session. It startled both of us and after apologising unreservedly, the client was able to witness me turning off my phone. We discussed the interruption and repair was possible within the room. Knowing how our hearing is heightened on the phone, I wonder how a similar experience would be managed during a phone therapy session. From that day forward, I switch off phones that I am not using for the call. I do this after the client has phoned for their appointment, in case we need a backup due to a technical failure.

Recording of the session inadvertently or deliberately

Since General Data Protection Regulation (GDPR) legislation, explicit consent must be sought following a clear explanation of why the call is being recorded, storage and sharing of data. Ethical therapy practice also requires explicit consent and adherence to GDPR requirements.

Confidentiality risks by various means include a third party having access to a client's phone and picking up a voicemail or seeing a text or first line of an email on a smartphone; call detail information on both land and mobile phones – date, duration, calling number, called number; call history on mobile and landlines – recently dialled, received, or unanswered calls.

Higher levels of risk

The BACP OPT competence framework (2021) states that therapists need knowledge of and the ability to discuss issues of confidentiality and data protection with clients and also wisely I think, that it is good practice to consider data security and privacy in relation to the client's individual circumstances and possible vulnerabilities. Depending on the client's circumstances and the level of risk, for example domestic abuse, in addition to talking over having sessions from a safe location, therapists might discuss phone safety measures such as turning off location sharing and checking advanced phone settings to bar unwanted people as administrators.

Discussions with clients presenting with high risk might include the following.

When the client phones the therapist:
- Use of 141 to withhold the last number called
- Last number redial – which can be cancelled on some phones
- Itemised phone bills

When the therapist phones the client:
- Call return – when 1471 is dialled, the client can hear the last number to call their number.
- Caller display/ID – the number that appears when you phone someone even if the call is not answered. It might also display the last few numbers the caller has made.

There might be times when risk presented by the client warrants knowledge of advanced smartphone security measures, for example tracking and geolocation. Further research and thought will be necessary and deliberating this in supervision is essential. It is important for therapists to be aware of the risks and use their informed judgement to evaluate sharing appropriate levels of security-related information with clients. This is the balancing act between safeguarding the client and terrifying them. If we think about privacy when you work face to face – an equivalent conversation with clients might be about whether your room was bugged, whether someone has their ear pressed against your counselling room door.

Assessing and managing risk requires reflection and is explored in Chapter 6. Risk cannot be avoided. There is no such thing as complete phone or online security and assessing risk can be more challenging when the client and therapist are not in the same room. That said, thinking through varies types of risk and how you will respond will better prepare you if and when a risk occurs.

When and how to contract

Informed consent

A written contract is considered to be a best practice as it allows the client to read and refer back to, if they want to clarify the terms of engagement, for example payment for a cancelled session. Although a verbal contract is equal to a written contract (Mitchels & Bond, 2011), obtaining written confirmation of understanding and consent is regarded as ethically and morally preferable for establishing and maintaining the therapeutic framework. The BACP Ethical Framework (2018) states that we will 'work with clients on the basis of their informed consent and agreement'.

Many written phone therapy contracts are now provided to clients online. This could be via a therapy service's own website with online forms and booking systems or web-based platforms providing email encryption, web forms and e-signatures such as DocuSign, Nitro Cloud, Hushmail and Egrit. Alternatively, individual therapists in private practice might send an email to clients with a contract attachment, with clients indicating explicit agreement by email reply.

Whatever method you use, don't lose sight of the need to provide equal access and be prepared to offer flexibility perhaps for older clients who are not tech-savvy or those with disabilities. If the initial contact with a client is over the phone, checking for accessibility and discussing alternatives can be done straight away. If an enquiry or referral was made electronically, a simple sentence about how to make contact to agree to alternative methods of consent can be included.

The first contact with clients

The offer of phone therapy might come from an individual therapist or organisation offering phone and or online therapy, perhaps a combination of phone, video, synchronous and/or asynchronous email therapy. Whatever therapy setting choices are on offer, I encourage you to start to validate phone therapy from the very first contact with clients. Communicate confidence about offering sessions via the phone – it has been providing effective therapy and treatment to clients for over 50 years. How you describe its efficacy and support your clients to access the benefits of the medium should begin with the very first contact you have with clients.

To give you some idea about how you might provide affirmation for phone therapy and manage any client apprehension, here is an extract from a first contact information sheet that I wrote for a counselling service:

> *Many people find counselling via the phone easier than they might have imagined, once they give it a try. The process of the work is just the same as face to face but with some differences that your counsellor will explain to you. Your counsellor will be able to guide you and discuss any uncertainties you might have about working on the phone when you first speak to each other or at a later stage if circumstances change.*
>
> *If privacy is a concern, your counsellor will consider this with you and support you to find a private space for sessions. This might include the use of earbuds, putting a radio by the door or being out of your home, perhaps in your car or outdoors, if this feels private enough for both of you.*
>
> *There are advantages to having counselling at a distance:*
>
> * *You are able to receive counselling at the comfort of your own home.*
> * *Some people find that it is easier to talk about personal issues on the phone when they're not seeing or being seen by their counsellor.*
> * *Some people find that it is easier to focus on what their counsellor is saying when they are not in the room together.*
>
> *On a practical level:*
> * *There are no travel and parking costs.*
> * *There is less of a time commitment to your weekly sessions as you won't need to factor in travel time getting to and from our offices.*

Having assured your client and gained willingness to proceed, the next stage will be to provide a working agreement for phone therapy.

Contracting with clients

It is always important to contract well with clients and working via the phone is no exception. The BACP Ethical Framework (2018) stresses the need for considered contracting 'We will give careful consideration to how we reach agreement with clients and will contract with them about the terms on which our services will be provided'. The framework states that we usually provide information to clients in advance so that they can make an informed decision about the therapy they want to receive.

When working via the phone, I find that the combination of sending written information for consideration in advance, followed by verbal confirmation and additional contracting during the first session, allows for ample opportunity for both parties to clarify the terms of their agreement. Sending your contract for discussion and agreement before therapy begins demonstrates respect for the client and your trustworthiness right from the start. When you contract, you have something to lean on if things don't go according to plan, and the time you spend contracting before entering into therapeutic work can help avoid having to sort any confusion later on. More information on contract law relating to therapy in general can be found in Bond (2015) and Mitchels and Bond (2011).

The BACP Good Practice in Action resource 'Making the contract in the counselling professions' (BACP, 2020) emphasises two components of a contract.

- The written element making up the 'business contract', including particulars around confidentiality, cancellations, payments and so on.
- The verbal element clarifies the 'therapeutic contract', how the therapist works, reviews, the client's part in the process.

While I agree that there are business and therapeutic elements, I prefer verbally confirming important written business elements during the first session and having some verbal therapeutic elements written into the contract.

Phone therapy contract with clients

Above all, it is important that a contract is easily understandable to the client. Just as with face-to-face therapy, how a contract is written will differ depending on context and personal preference. When I train therapists who work in therapy services, I encourage them to think about the content of their organisation's written contract and consider whether they would like to add any additional, verbally negotiated boundaries between themselves and their clients.

The content of a phone therapy contract will have similar elements to a face-to-face contract but with some differences included such as the following.

Arrangements for telephone sessions

I start my contract with practical arrangements to set the scene for therapy by phone. This section includes:

Who will initiate the call at the agreed session time

To try to avoid clients phoning early – there is no virtual waiting room – I reiterate the importance of phoning at the agreed time in my email confirming the session.

Privacy

I ask that clients make arrangements to ensure that they won't be disturbed during their session. This is the starting point for a discussion and perhaps negotiation during the first session about what you both feel constitutes a private setting. More on privacy can be found later.

How technical problems will be handled

Typically, this will be by sending a text or an email if the technical issue is the client's or by therapists using another phone if the problem is theirs. I discuss this verbally with clients during the first session as arrangements might need to be different according to personal circumstances. A word of caution – a phone line going dead might signal a breach of privacy for your client. How this will be handled will need to be discussed with your clients.

Session frequency, length and timeframe

This will be usually the same as face to face, for example weekly, 50-minute sessions for four weeks in the first instance and then review or for six weeks for example if the work is short term.

Phone therapy only or blended

If both parties agree to a blended approach in the first instance, contracting matters relating to face to face, video- or text-based therapy can be included. If phone therapy transitions to face to face or other media, re-contracting is a good practice.

Appropriateness of phone therapy for the client

My contract states that if I believe that phone therapy is not suitable for or not proving of benefit to the client, I will discuss this with them and support them to access a more appropriate help.

Boundary-related requests

Boundary matters can also be included in the written contract, for example 'On the day of your session, please avoid alcoholic drinks and recreational drugs'. Or, 'Please don't smoke or eat during your session'. These and other boundary issues are usually hotly debated on my training course and you will have your own views including whether to negotiate boundaries verbally instead of including them in the written contract.

Out-of-session contact

There will be times when it is necessary to make contact, to cancel a session for example, but most therapists will want to be explicit about the need to limit communication between themselves and the client outside of the therapeutic frame.

Non-recording agreement

In the interests of trust and good faith, sessions won't be recorded and that any request or need to record sessions will be openly discussed and agreed in writing.

Confidentiality

A contract should have an explanation about keeping records such as session notes and contact details in accordance with GDPR legislation, sharing clinical material in supervision, having a clinical will, limits to confidentiality and under what circumstances you will disclose information. This will usually be if you believe that there is a risk of harm to self and others and will include who you will disclose information to, as well as the specifics of what it means to be working in accordance with the law. There are legal exceptions to holding in confidence what clients disclose, for example if you were compelled to do so by a court order. The Terrorism Act of 2000 provides a duty to disclose to the police any knowledge or suspicion of terrorism as soon as possible and the Drug Trafficking Act of 1994 requires we disclose information of any drug money laundering or suspicion of it. It is a criminal offence not to do so and it is also an offence to let the client know of our actions. Knowing when and why we need to report safeguarding concerns is essential. This means knowing the difference between a legal obligation, any duty to report (organisational protocols for instance) and moral or ethical reason that you would consider in supervision. These matters will be much the same as the face-to-face setting, and full information on this is well documented by the major professional therapy bodies. What will be different regarding confidentiality in a phone therapy setting is how not being physically present with a client will be managed. The starting point will be obtaining the contact details of a person the client chooses to be an emergency contact along with GP details. More on risk and how times of emergency can be managed will be considered in Chapter 6.

Payment of fees

As payment in person will not be possible, other methods such as automated bank payments – PayPal, Worldpay, Shopify, Handepay, BACS in the UK – or any of other growing number of online payment services should be included. Consider your terms – will you require payment in advance? Will sessions take place if payment isn't received? Payment for therapy can be a highly emotive issue and each therapist will hold their own view on this. My contract requests that clients pay in advance for sessions, and I address non-payment by email reminder in the first instance, during the week before the next session. Clarity and frank discussion are important but take care, technology glitches do occur so without being able to see how a query about non-payment is received by a client, a gentle reminder is preferable to risk shaming them and a possible rupturing to the work.

> *A client phoned early for his session, and I wasn't able to answer his call. The client then emailed saying he assumed I didn't pick up because he didn't pay in advance for his session as he was in a rush that day. Even though I replied to the client soon after I received his email and explained that the session was scheduled in my dairy at a later time, that I wasn't available to pick up the phone before the appointment, that I would never refuse to take a call if a client hadn't paid in advance and that I was available for him to call me during the remainder of his session – the client did not phone again. The client didn't reply to my email for a number of days. Fortunately, another appointment was eventually agreed, and we had a chance to discuss what had occurred. This gave us the opportunity to explore the client's fear of rejection and abandonment as well as practical issues around payment.*

Cancellation of sessions and non-attendance

Commitment to counselling and cancellation can be another sensitive issue. Be unambiguous about your cancellation policy – any offer to rearrange over a certain number of days, under what circumstances and when the full fee will be payable. Also, explain what will happen if you need to cancel a session. Non-attendance also needs to be thought through. How long will you be available if the client doesn't phone or if the client doesn't answer the call? Would your availability be any different when you are trying to call the client as opposed to waiting for them to call? Many therapy services that call clients for sessions have a policy of trying a certain number of times within a timeframe; for instance, three unanswered calls within a 20-minute period would constitute a DNA. Whatever you decide, transparent communication about expectations and commitment is key.

Professional code of ethics

Confirmation of the professional body or bodies that you are registered with and an explanation of how you work in accordance with their code of ethics is a necessity. Information about where the client can find out more and contact the body for advice should they need this is important; however, stating your intention to discuss any problems that might occur between you can go a long way to resolving any misunderstandings.

Legal considerations

Insurance

Most professional bodies will require therapists to hold adequate and current insurance if they are working with clients in a professional capacity and informing clients of this is part of the contracting procedure. Public liability is required to cover you should a client suffer injury of some sort if they come to your premises. Professional indemnity insurance is needed in case you are sued for negligence or malpractice by a client and good cover is essential for all phone therapists. If you are employed by or are on placement within an organisation, it is likely that insurance will be provided but check that this covers phone therapy as well as face-to-face therapy. If you are in private practice, shop around the growing number of insurance policies for therapist providers. Consider the context of your practice, perhaps you are working with young people or vulnerable adults and choose a level of cover suitable for the level of risk. Make sure that phone therapy is included – if the policy states online therapy, check that this includes the phone. Take care to check any changes in policy cover relating to working on the phone before you renew your cover.

Working internationally

As phone and indeed online therapy offers such accessibility and flexibility, it is tempting to think that a fully international practice is possible. New clients might approach you if you specialise, existing clients might move abroad or indeed you might travel internationally and want to continue working. Unfortunately, it is not as simple as it seems. Precisely where remote therapy occurs – the location from which it is supplied or where it is received – has been debated for years.

Anthony (2014) cautions us by saying that just because we are able to work with clients in different countries, it doesn't mean that we are legally or ethically positioned to do so.

> There is no central database of what is allowable country by country, and while this is yet to be tested in a court of law it is our remit as professionals to remain as up to date as possible in a global capacity as to 'where' we may practise.
>
> (2014, p. 39)

Some countries and states in the United States have licensing regulations which allow therapists to practice only within their physical borders. Different legal systems protect the use of professional titles and providing therapy without being registered or licensed in that country can be a criminal offence.

The Association for Counselling and Therapy Online (ACTO) raises some important points, including that qualifications are not always recognised in other countries. ACTO's website states that psychotherapists registered with the UKCP, being the National Accrediting Organisation (NAO) for the UK, can work throughout Europe by applying to the European Association of Psychotherapy (EAP) for a European Certificate of Psychotherapy (ECP).

> This is the nearest thing to a 'passport' for psychotherapists within Europe (generally). It can help in getting accreditation in another EAP-NAO across Europe – from Ireland to Russia. However, it doesn't carry a huge weight with health services etc or, at this stage, give a right to work in another country.
>
> ACTO (2021)

If you decide to offer phone therapy internationally, then do your research into the law, regulations as well as gauging mental health provision in the client's country. This should flag obvious prohibiting factors. It is now generally agreed that if a therapist and client are located in different countries, then two different legal systems, subject to different laws, will come into play. Consider speaking to your insurance company's helpline, although they might not be able to give advice on specific countries. Include a clause on working internationally in your contract. Clearly state that the therapy is being provided in accordance with the laws of the practitioner's own country and any disputes will be subject to that country's law. If you are working from the UK, make sure you state the applicable country's law – England, Scotland, Wales and Northern Ireland. A clause is not absolute protection against litigation, so weigh up the risks to your clients and your practice.

Another consideration of working internationally is being aware of multicultural considerations beyond awareness of race and culture within our own country.

Leong and Ponterotto (2003) and Leong and Blustein (2000) call for the need to move beyond a national multicultural perspective towards a global vision of counselling psychology. The idea being that therapy training should include training elements on different worldviews. I suspect that internationalising therapy will be discussed further as digital therapy becomes more commonplace and perspectives on race, culture and difference for phone therapy are explored in Chapter 7 on EDI.

GDPR

If you work in the UK, making it clear about compliance to General Data Protection Regulation (GDPR) and the Data Protection Act (2018) should form an intrinsic part of your contract and explicit consent must be sought from clients. Whether you work on the phone, online or as face-to-face therapist, if you collect or store data, on a device or on paper, you are obliged to register with the Information Commissioner's Office (ICO) (2018). Clients need to be made aware of the lawful basis for keeping and using personal information as well as for how long you store information when therapy ends, where you store client's data – electronic and paper, whether you share information with third-party contacts, the client's right to access data you collect about them and if you have a website, how your site collects and processes information. Certain types of data breach must be reported to the ICO, but even with minor breaches of confidentiality, in the spirit of transparency and honesty, being open with clients and apologising for minor breaches before logging as part of your own GDPR processes is a good practice. The ICO www.ico.org.uk provides full details on GDPR compliance and the BACP, UKCP and BPS have information on how to work legally with clients.

With a carefully considered, robust therapy contract in place, the framework to support for the first session is in place.

The first session

The first session and assessment process in therapy vary widely. Practices and procedures in therapy services and in private practice differ. Some practitioners and services will collect pre-assessment information, some therapists prefer as little information as possible in advance while some clients have an assessment session before being allocated a different therapist. The assessment might be the first session, or the first session might be the start of a staged assessment process.

Whatever the therapy context, process or modality, when we work on the phone or indeed online, we also assess the suitability of the medium for the client on an individual basis. The BACP OPT competence framework (2021) states that a client's 'ability to make safe and effective use of OPT needs to be assessed prior to starting therapy and periodically throughout the process'. We need to assess the client's access to and ability to use technology. Fortunately, the phone is a medium that has a high level of accessibility and has fewer challenges than video and email therapy for clients with little technical knowledge. We also need to consider what the OPT competence framework describes as the client's 'ability to engage in a therapeutic relationship and express their feelings, situation and experience remotely'.

First session, first contact

Without sight, it is imperative that the first few seconds and minutes of verbal communication are focused on putting your client at ease. Being prepared for the call is essential. Having a thought through process of engagement and assessment, knowing what you will say and what information you require will allow you to relax and focus on listening to your client. Talking with a calm, reassuring tone of voice is the starting point for building trust and rapport with the client.

Who will initiate the call?

In over 13 years of training therapists, I have found that more individual practitioners prefer clients to phone them to replicate face-to-face therapy and the majority of therapy services opt to phone clients. There is no right or wrong in this regard. I ask my clients to phone me because I feel it shows their commitment to therapy, they can decide not to call if their privacy is unexpectedly breached. Also, I don't have to bear the cost of any call charges.

When the client calls the therapist

Be prepared for the call. It sounds obvious, but when I first started to work on the phone, readying myself, checking my appearance and the room for a face-to-face session was replaced by a visual void that tricked me into fitting in just one more task on my to-do list before the client called. Feeling rushed when the phone rang, I soon learnt my lesson. I created a pre-session routine that allows me to answer the phone unhurriedly, breathing evenly and with a clear virtual headspace to meet my client.

Maxine Rosenfield (1997) suggests letting the phone ring three times before answering. This allows anxious clients enough time to process that your phone is ringing. When a client calls me for the first time, I answer on the third ring and say 'Hello, Sarah speaking'. The client knows that I have answered the call and it serves as an invitation for them to say, 'Hello, this is . . .', after which I welcome them warmly to the session. Immediately after this, I ask the client whether they are in a private location.

When the counsellor calls the client

Assuming that the client doesn't say their name when they answer, check that they are indeed the client as opposed to someone else answering the phone. Once you've established that you're speaking to the client and you've identified yourself, move directly on to checking the client's privacy by asking if they are alone and free to talk to you now. The key difference between the client calling you and you calling the client is that you cannot be sure that even with their best intentions, privacy might have been breached. If they were calling you, they would have had control of their environment to delay until they were private once more.

If you are calling from a therapy service to arrange a convenient appointment time for the first session, make sure you make this clear as soon as possible after your introduction and the privacy check. The client's need to talk and the effect of disinhibition – not seeing you trying to interject – could mean that they launch into material which you then have to close down, potentially leaving them emotionally vulnerable.

Verbal contracting and boundary setting

After meeting your client in voice and checking their privacy, the beginning of the first session is an opportunity to reiterate the written contract, which they are likely to have received in advance. This might include talking through limits to confidentiality, your cancellation policy and how technical issues will be dealt with.

Technical issues and boundary setting

Agreeing to how technical problems will be managed will differ depending on the client's circumstances as well as how the therapist works. Poor reception is annoying but will be obvious to you both. Simply ending the call and phoning again often takes care of glitches. If problems persist, you might agree that you would end a mobile data or landline call and move to Wi-Fi calling, being mindful of all the data security matters covered earlier. I usually train groups of therapists on a teleconference line and welcome technical issues when they occur. I explain that our training environment mirrors phone therapy with the client and that getting comfortable with technical faults and handling them collectively will reassure the client and help them take the unexpected in their stride. Know that glitches can and will occur – it is how you manage them that matters.

What if the line goes dead? Some therapy services whose therapists phone clients for sessions have a policy that they will not call again if the call ends suddenly as they can't be sure that the client hasn't put the phone down hastily due to a privacy breach. This boundary will have been explained to the client as part of contracting, and a follow-up email or message will be sent to obtain consent to call again or rearrange the appointment. As my clients phone me, I agree that they will call me back, so that I can be sure they are still able to talk freely. Discuss and agree safe and practical next steps with clients to avoid anxiety and the client potentially feeling rejected or abandoned if you decide not to call them back.

Some thoughts about privacy

Drawing the client's attention to having a session in private starts in the written contract and is spoken about in the first session and sometimes frequently beyond this. For some clients, checking and assessing privacy is part and parcel of every session. What constitutes a private space can look very different from one client to another, which is why we shouldn't assume understanding and ask questions relevant to the clients' personal circumstances. I have found that agreeing to an appropriate setting is best done by negotiation with some clients and helping others to troubleshoot if their setting is not ideal.

> *A long-term client took extended lunch hour once a week and phoned me from her car felt private to us both. Another client phoned from a queue at the bank as this felt private to her but didn't feel either private enough or conducive to the work of therapy to me.*
>
> *My work with young people on the phone, particularly during the Coronavirus pandemic lockdowns included agreeing to creative solutions and privacy trial-and-error testing such as building a wall of pillows and cushions to make a soundproof pod in bedrooms. Having a session during a permitted daily exercise walk proved to be a suitable time and space for therapy for some young people. However, going to the shop for mum with a younger*

sibling in tow was not. See Chapter 7 for more on working with children and young people.

Sessions outdoors can be effective. Outdoors can include anything from walking therapy, sitting in the middle of a field or in a garden shed. I am cautious about sessions in the garden though as wooden garden wall panels and hedges can create an illusion of privacy. Gardens can vary in size and the voice of someone talking outside a terrace house can be carried a few doors down. Having said that, what clients see when they are outdoors might form part of the work and even become a useful metaphor. A client sitting in her car working through a painful divorce described feeling held by the darkness and guided by the light of Jupiter clearly visible to her in the night sky.

Therapy by phone can allow us a thought-provoking insight into the client's world that isn't afforded to us when we work in the therapy room.

During a first session with a new adult client, I heard someone come into earshot and call out, 'Hello' before starting to talk about work. The client quickly responded 'I'm on the phone' in what I experienced as a soft, appeasing tone. When I checked privacy with her and asked whether she would like to end and arrange another session, she quickly said, 'Yes please'. We emailed to agree to a mutually convenient time, and I followed up what had occurred in the next session. The client said her partner had known her session time but entered the room and started a conversation, nevertheless. This gave me a first-hand experience of their relationship and how they communicated in a way that would not have occurred if I was in face-to-face therapy with the client. She was able to talk about her previously unspoken frustration and she shared that the interruption during her session time made her more aware of her feelings about her partner's behaviour. We discussed how she might claim privacy for herself during and outside of sessions.

When a privacy breach isn't obvious

Keep your ear cocked for noise in the client's background and any change in their behaviour that might indicate a change. Was there a pause mid-sentence, did they hesitate in a way that wasn't connected to the material of the session or has the client started to give one-word answers? If you sense a change, bring it up by asking the client a closed question to establish if they are no longer alone. Agreeing an 'alert word' or 'safe phrase' with clients during contracting in advance is a simple way for them to let you know that privacy has been breached. I think this can be extremely useful for vulnerable clients who are at risk.

My client chose a fruit for the 'alert word' she would use to signal to me if ever her therapy was interrupted by another person. Fortunately, she never had cause to say 'kiwi' during a session, but the idea of a code word as means of communication appealed to her beyond her sessions. Having PTSD, she experienced triggers leading her to feeling panic, fear, hypervigilance, intrusive thoughts, irritability and tearfulness. By sharing her 'alert word' with her partner, she could let him know that she had been triggered. He was able to give her what she needed at that moment, and she was able to focus on grounding exercises without having to explain herself.

Regarding therapist privacy

The intrusion of any noise in your room, another phone ringing or email pinging will feel greater to your client than if it happened face to face – they might imagine that you are not fully present with them while you check messages. If I'm ever disturbed, I tell the client what has occurred. I let my clients know about any background noises for instance, road works or a neighbour's noisy garden equipment, as I am aware that just as my hearing will be heightened, so too will my client's. Stating what is going on in the background can avoid a puzzled or startled client, and I can put the annoyance of the sound to one side, relax and tune into my client.

Turn off any notifications on your phone during a client session. Emails, instant messages, office assistants, software update alerts and the like are all distracting for a few moments. The client will hear them too and a beep creates extra work as you both refocus after privacy was encroached upon.

Contracting privacy

When I train therapists, I suggest they reflect on their own experience, preferences and any disability when they contract with clients. Contracting privacy might involve asking the client not to use speakerphone, not to eat or drink during sessions or to not do other things when they have their session – like driving, emptying the dishwasher or some other multitasking activity.

Therapy services contracts are likely to include asking the client to make sure they are located in a private setting where they won't be disturbed. You might like to consider your own privacy contract with clients which sits alongside the service's which might be verbally agreeing to boundaries such as those discussed earlier.

Ending the first and subsequent sessions

Towards the end of the session, especially if the client has disclosed a lot of material, I start to virtually time keep. I might let the client know that we have about ten minutes or five minutes until the session ends. Setting and holding a time boundary on the phone and online is particularly important for clients who might find disengaging and post session self-care difficult. To help with this, I allow time at the end of the first session to discuss the difference between ending a face-to-face and phone session. I explain that if we were in a room together there would be time for them to put on their coat, pick up their bag, walk to their car or the bus stop and how all of this helps their re-entry into the world outside the therapy room. I then describe how in a short while we will say goodbye, the phone line will become silent and they will be alone with themselves. As the end of a phone session can feel abrupt, my aim is to suggest an ending routine for clients which, depending on their circumstances, might include sitting quietly in their room to avoid immediate contact with others in the home or making a hot drink and sitting awhile or walking outdoors or drawing or writing – whatever works best for the client.

The UKCP Guidelines for working online or remotely (2021) say that there can be 'significant benefits to the lack of a physical journey and the comfort a client may feel being in their own setting'. Also, they offer an interesting suggestion. Pointing out that clients could be less prepared for their session when there is no physical journey to the therapy room, they propose agreeing to a boundary for the session, one idea being 'to suggest to clients that they "travel" to the session, even if that is walking up and down the stairs, and the same to "travel" home'.

Whatever arrival and ending boundary or ritual you and your client decide upon is up to you, what is key when we work remotely is to create a conscious ending. Having set the scene for self-care at the end of the initial session, I remind the client of the ending routine particularly if they experience a difficult session in the future. When sessions are particularly challenging, I take time to ground the client – more on this can be found in Chapter 8.

References

ACTO. (2021, June 30). *International*. www.acto.org.uk/info-for-public/acto-international/

Anthony, K. (2014). Training therapists to work effectively online and offline within digital culture. *British Journal of Guidance & Counselling, 43*(1), 36–42. https://doi.org/10.10 80/03069885.2014.924617

BACP. (2018). *BACP ethical framework for the counselling professions*. www.bacp.co.uk/ media/3103/bacp-ethical-framework-for-the-counselling-professions-2018.pdf

BACP. (2020, June). *BACP good practice in action 055 fact sheet: Making the contract in the counselling professions*. www.bacp.co.uk/events-and-resources/ethics-and-standards/ good-practice-in-action/publications/gpia055-making-the-contract-fs/

BACP Online and Phone Therapy (OPT) competence framework. (2021). www.bacp. co.uk/media/10849/bacp-online-and-phone-therapy-competence-framework-feb21.pdf

Balick, A. (2012). TMI in the transference LOL: Psychoanalytic reflections on Google, social networking, and 'virtual impingement'. *Psychoanalysis, Culture & Society, 17*(2), 120–136. https://doi.org/10.1057/pcs.2012.19

Balick, A. (2017). *Ask an expert: Why you need a digital policy, BACP private practice, spring 2017*. www.bacp.co.uk/bacp-journals/private-practice/spring-2017/ ask-an-expert/

Bond, T. (2015). *Standards and ethics for counselling in action (counselling in action series)* (Rev. ed.). SAGE.

ICO. (2018). *Guide to data protection*. https://ico.org.uk/for-organisations/guide-to-data-protection/

Leong, F. T. L., & Blustein, D. L. (2000). Toward a global vision of counseling psychology. *The Counseling Psychologist, 28*(1), 5–9. https://doi.org/10.1177/0011000000281001

Leong, F. T. L., & Ponterotto, J. G. (2003). A proposal for internationalizing counseling psychology in the United States. *The Counseling Psychologist, 31*, 381–395.

Mitchels, B., & Bond, T. (2011). *Legal issues across counselling & psychotherapy settings: A guide for practice (legal resources counsellors & psychotherapists)* (1st ed.). SAGE.

Rosenfield, M. (1997). *Counselling by telephone (professional skills for counsellors series)* (1st ed.). SAGE.

UKCP. (2021). *UKCP guidelines for working online or remotely*. www.psychotherapy.org.uk/media/jrohoner/ukcp-guidelines-for-working-online-or-remotely-v1-0.pdf

Chapter 6

Assessment, psychological suitability and risk

The phone therapy assessment

A phone therapy assessment is a balancing act. We aim to find the balance between undertaking a well-considered assessment that is appropriate for the client, while at the same time being aware of the need to connect with and start building a relationship with the client without being able to see them.

Without your body language to soften your enquiry and information gathering, a rigid process risks leaving the client feeling assessed rather than working with you to decide whether your offer of phone therapy is appropriate for them.

The BACP OPT competence framework (2021) states that therapists need 'an ability to judge the level of information required in an assessment, based on the level of risk being presented and levels of support available to the client'. This is useful guidance on how to maintain the balance – we use our clinical judgement to determine the level of information required in the first session against the degree of risk and support systems already in place for each individual client.

Standard mental health questionnaires, for example CORE outcome measures, GAD7 – Anxiety, PHQ 9 – Depression, can also be used during phone therapy. These may be helpful for assessing and monitoring risk but give some thought to how this will be done when you are not in the room with the client. Although evidence-based information might be regarded as a less intrusive method of gauging risk at least initially – without sight, reading a long questionnaire to a client on the phone can feel like an interrogation. Consider whether questionnaires could be sent to the client electronically for completion before or after the first session or during the work when necessary. While I understand the necessity for questionnaires to flag risk, monitor levels of client distress or 'improvement' or to provide an audit of services, I often hear how therapists struggle to incorporate monitoring without it feeling invasive, particularly in short-term phone therapy. Perhaps, there is a need for therapy services to review the linchpin between verbal use of questionnaires, level of risk and the need to develop and maintain a relationship with the client during phone therapy.

A phone therapy assessment is broadly similar to the face-to-face process with some key differences relating to not seeing or being physically present with the client, particularly in cases of risk.

DOI: 10.4324/9781003253396-6

Client identity and contact details

Being mindful of the need to connect with the client and start building a relationship as quickly as possible while at the same time needing to consider safety when working at a distance, I prefer to obtain the following information before inviting the client to tell me why they have come for therapy, some of which might be collected before the first session.

- Working remotely requires that we need to establish the identity of the client. This means we obtain the client's name, age, address, home phone, mobile number and email address. Just as with face to face, in line with GDPR legislation, ask the client for permission to call them, leave messages and email them when necessary. Depending on how the client answers, if they sound anxious and issues of risk arise, discuss how risk and client safety will be managed when you are not in the same room – more on this later in this chapter.
- In addition to their personal and contact details, it is also best practice to collect the client's GP name and address, making it clear about whether you will routinely contact their doctor and what information you will disclose or whether contact with their GP will occur only if risk emerges. Sharing your policy and practices around circumstances for breaking confidentiality even though the client might have received this as part of your written contract allows time for discussion and talk around any client concern about breaking confidentiality before they share information with you.
- An emergency contact that the client gives permission for you to contact in times of emergency. The UKPC's online or remote guidelines (2021) suggest you ask the client for a 'safety contact' – someone who they trust and who knows they are in therapy with you. I think this term is caring and less emotive than mentioning emergencies or a crisis. This might be a friend or a family member. Agree with the client how this individual will be told as you will be storing their data such as their phone number.

Adapting your face-to-face assessment process for phone therapy

At the beginning of the first session, I verbally discuss key written business- and boundary-related elements from my contract. With contractual, contact details and practicalities covered first, I am able to move on to a more open style of assessment, listening to the client, telling them I will manage the time and come back to any additional information I might need towards the end of the session. This gives the client space to be heard and me the flexibility to assert a time boundary to return to any avenue of potential risk at the end if the client has revealed this as part of their sharing.

Assessment processes vary according to therapist modality, style, experience and client group. Some therapists prefer a series of direct questions contained within a single session after which, subsequent sessions are unstructured for the client to use as they wish. Other therapists use a continuous assessment approach, and some use a four-session assessment model. It is up to you to consider working without seeing your client and deciding how and to what degree you will adapt your face-to-face assessment process to work on the phone.

Typically, a phone therapy assessment will incorporate the following information

- The presenting issues, why the client has come for therapy and why now
- Health-related information, how the client regards their health, including diagnoses of mental health and physical illnesses. If they are receiving medical care including support from mental health teams and whether these professionals know they are seeking therapy
- Any medication, why this has been prescribed, how it makes the client feel
- The client's key relationships and support systems
- Any alcohol or drug use
- Any history of self-harm
- Any suicidal ideation, now or in the past
- Any previous experience of therapy, what worked and didn't work for them
- What they hope to gain from therapy
- Any preferences for the work together – topics, techniques, methods

Two additional phone therapy assessment questions you might like to include are

- *What attracted you to phone therapy?*

  If you offer generic therapy as opposed to therapy related to a specific issue, a client might choose phone therapy because they have mobility difficulties, agoraphobia, suffer from social anxiety or don't have access to transport. Whatever the reason, this information will be useful for the work.

- *Is there anything else you would like to tell me about yourself – perhaps something that is related to the fact that we can't see each other?*

  You might consider prompting the client by way of examples, for instance 'Some clients might mention how they look, their race, something about their culture or gender identity or disability perhaps' (useful suggestions from specialist therapists on assessment questions and EDI can be found in Chapter 7).

This question has been invaluable to me. From the very first session it has helped me to avoid assumptions with some clients and gain important information outside of what I would usually hope for during an assessment with others. I have noticed that it also reaches clients in different ways as sometimes they offer material that has nothing whatever to do with not being seen by me but about themselves which I might have needed to wait a few sessions for or possibly even never shared.

This raises an interesting point. What if the client doesn't want to share information that is hidden to us without seeing them but which we would regard as important in their lives and relevant to the therapy – a physical disability perhaps? Our desire to fully understand the challenges and context of the client's life to be of use to them might be at odds with the client's longing or need to present themselves unencumbered by their physical presence. Phone therapy allows them the freedom of physical anonymity. Perhaps, for the first time, the client can experience non-judgemental positive regard without it being related to how they look or present themselves. This circumstance could be viewed as an example of invisibility as understood as an element of the online disinhibition effect (Suler, 2004). On the other hand, perhaps, phone therapy can allow a client just to be, even if it is only for a short while before their material leads them to disclose all of what we immediately see in the therapy room.

Whatever your preferred assessment method or the process of assessment required by the therapy service you work within, what will be the same for all therapists is the ethical obligation to work within our professional competence. Talking about your revised phone therapy assessment process with your supervisor might help you notice potential weaknesses. This will be particularly true for newly qualified therapists as in the absence of experience, drawing on the knowledge of those with a higher level of competence and skill can help safeguard your clients and yourself.

As you take stock of your assessment process, I suggest you bear the following in mind

CLIENT DISINHIBITION

Without seeing your response, it is possible for a distressed client who has been waiting for their first session with you to fill the entire hour singlehandedly. An unstructured session could leave you without even the most basic contact details and the client with a sense of having offloaded without boundaries to someone unknown to them and perhaps feeling exposed, vulnerable or ashamed after the call. For some therapists, this might be a reason to have a more structured assessment process on the phone than when working face to face.

SESSION TIME MANAGEMENT

Disinhibition without visuals can result in feeling that time passes very quickly for both client and therapist. In phone therapy we don't have a clock in the room either for your client to notice or for you to glance at as a way of keeping note of the time; instead, we use a virtual clock by letting the client know how much session time they have left. During an assessment session you might like to offer a verbal timeframe to your client which might be letting them know how many minutes they have to tell you why they have come for therapy. This can allow them the freedom to express themselves while you are able to listen attentively during that time without being distracted by time management worry.

Assessing risk

Assessing risk when not physically present with a client can be more ambiguous than when working face to face with a client. Assessing non-verbal cues that might signal distress or vulnerability might mean it is harder to discern the level of risk and without being in the room together, there is a limit to how much you can intervene if risk occurs. How can we hold this knowledge in mind and make provision to work ethically as phone therapists?

To appraise risk in phone therapy, we need a framework comprising the following

A robust written contract which has been verbally discussed with clients. They have consented to the terms of the therapy contract and how you will work together. Any additional boundaries have been negotiated and agreed with the client as part of the assessment process.

An assessment process which encompasses consideration of:

- the setting – where the client is located and the level of privacy afforded to them;
- security and safety regarding equipment and technology – access to their own phone, awareness around location sharing, privacy regarding call history and the like;
- client's personal circumstances – for example the threat of domestic abuse or obstruction from a third party; and
- client's physical and mental health – any diagnoses, treatment, medication. Any history of self-harming or suicidal indication or plans.

This is the point at which we consider the client's psychological suitability for phone therapy and our own level of competence.

Assessment is the process which helps us make a judgement call about a client's mental health, whether we feel they are psychologically minded enough, if we feel sufficiently skilled to work with them and whether we feel therapy can take place on the phone. It's reasonable to allow yourself and clients a longer assessment process when risk becomes evident during the first session. In the spirit of wanting to make sure that what you are able to offer as well as assessing if the medium of the phone is right for the client, an additional session can be arranged which will give you time to reflect, discuss the client, with your supervisor, undertake some research about the presenting issue and consider additional boundaries or contractual agreements to safeguard the client. This might include an initial period of ongoing assessment, perhaps of four to six sessions, to allow for the emergence and identification of specific difficulties followed by clear contractual understandings in case there is a problem beyond this timeframe.

The decision not to continue past the assessment can be spoken about in the session in the spirit of wanting to help the client access the most appropriate support, whether this is about the timing of therapy, working with a different therapist or receiving a more medical approach. The client might feel that the phone setting isn't practical or just doesn't feel right for them. Equally, it might be your clinical and ethical view that phone therapy isn't appropriate for them. Both views are valid and should be respected.

In my experience most clients are willing to work cooperatively when I suggest we have another session to give us time to explore certain aspects further before committing to working together. I have found that suggesting this additional time builds trust and provides a strong foundation for the work. I have experienced only one case when this has not been possible. The client became extremely angry when I asked about alcohol use, suspecting that drinking had occurred before and during the session. The client had not approached me for addiction or substance misuse therapy, her reason was related to living apart from a child. This client flatly refused another session and in spite of my best attempts to talk about the impact of alcohol on our ability to work with the pain of estrangement, sadly no further appointment was made. I sent follow-up emails to the client expressing my willingness to arrange a session to discuss how we might work together at a later point, should she want this.

In cases of risk, asking why the client wants therapy via phone at this time and why they chose you will give you further information about whether it might be possible to work together. What are they hoping for? Is this realistic? Therapy goals, aims or focus are useful for gauging the client's capacity to understand and engage in phone therapy. Asking questions about how you might work together, what they would like in the work, what wouldn't be helpful, whether they have any preferences – will provide further information on the client's cognitive ability in cases that present risk.

Positive risk-taking

Just like data security, where absolutely security does not exist, the same is true when it comes to client risk. It is highly improbable that clients are likely to be free of risk, the reality is that we have to accept that risk is present all the time in therapy whether this is in a face-to-face, online or phone therapy setting. It is helpful to consider Reeves (2015), who writes about positive risk-taking. Reeves (2021) is clear that positive risk-taking is not the same as being passive or doing nothing, as this would be negligent, 'if we accept that risk is present in all therapy, we can instead see it as part of the frame; something to be actively worked with in collaboration with our clients'.

Working collaboratively with clients, recognising and exploring risk, then supporting them to manage risk instead of trying to eliminate or avoid it is a much more realistic approach. It is a natural fit for phone therapy where without visual cues, we take care to avoid making assumptions, we ask more open questions, we work with clients more synergistically.

Assessment of psychological suitability for phone therapy

The BACP OPT competence framework (2021) states that we need an ability to assess clients for psychological suitability, considering if they need a high level of care and support, are struggling to function, present a high level of risk (e.g. suicide, self-harm), evidence poor reality testing, are resistant to the imposition of appropriate boundaries, exhibit or describe relational difficulties which may possibly be heightened by the environment of online or phone therapy or present in a fragmented and inconsistent manner online or on the phone.

At first glance, this list of vulnerable presentations can cause anxiety. Indeed, when I train therapists, many often exclaim that most of their clients present in these ways, and they question whether working on the phone is ethical in these circumstances. It is important to note that the requirement is to assess for phone and online settings on a client-by-client basis, not refuse to work with them unless in a face-to-face setting.

My view is that all of the aforementioned are considerations for *any* assessment session or a subsequent session, whether working face to face or on the phone, video or by text.

A starting point for assessing psychological suitability is to ask yourself about what you would do if you were physically present with the client. If you would not work with a client in a face-to-face setting, it is likely to be because to do so would be outside of your level of competence or because you believe the client needs a different type of therapy, intervention or other support that neither you and/or your therapy service can provide. To ask yourself, 'If I would work with this client face to face, why specifically wouldn't I work with them on the phone?' allows you to consider suitability from a rational, ethical base. It will help you tease out precisely why the medium of the phone is inappropriate for the client at this time.

In my experience, the phone can become the scapegoat for issues that are more about the therapist's general level of experience, competence or what might be the most appropriate treatment for a client. Some years ago, a manager from an employee assistance programme (EAP) told me that therapist anxiety was often levelled at phone and after exploration, it became clear that issues of psychological suitability were more about whether short-term, solution-focused therapy was appropriate for the client rather than the medium of the phone. I suspect that the exponential growth of phone-delivered EAP therapy since then has given rise to greater practitioner confidence and expertise in the medium.

That said, part of the assessment process is also an opportunity to make sure that we are working within our competence as we need to consider our ethical duty of care to our clients and ourselves. It is neither ethical nor wise to work with clients if we don't have adequate training and knowledge. We are obliged to review our continuing professional development needs and undertake training to support working safely and effectively on the phone.

In line with most other aspects of phone therapy we aim for a collaborative approach when we gauge risk. Communicating more actively to explore risk, being frank about the need for this by leaning on the fact that we can't see the client – that we're not in the room together – can help us ask for information that we need to assess safeguarding matters.

I agree with Hawkins and Shohet (2012) when he says, 'Any action or thought that springs from fear is ultimately unproductive'. Notice your own process and work reflexively throughout the assessment – use your thoughts, feelings, beliefs, responses to inform your choices and actions regarding working with the client.

Aim to relax and tune in to what your client is saying, their vocal presentation – tone, speed, pitch, intonation. How are they linking sentences? One of the key indicators for suitability is the client's capacity to engage in the assessment, whether they are able to participate in communicating with you so that you're having a two-way conversation. Are they capable of stopping to listen to you? Are you noticing incessant, running away talking which isn't linear, during which the client is going off on tangents or rants? Observe silences, are they reflective, do they make sense within your communication together or are there long pauses which feel like the client is either unable or unwilling to communicate.

There could be a number of reasons why a client presents in these ways which need to be explored, but if the client discloses that they have a serious mental health condition, getting the full understanding of this by asking questions, such as who diagnosed this, when and what treatment they are receiving and whether other professionals involved know they are seeking counselling, will help inform your decision to either work with the client on the phone or indeed in any other setting.

Managing risk in times of crisis

Suicidal ideation and self-harm

Perhaps, the risk which causes the greatest worry for therapists who work on the phone is a client expressing suicidal thoughts or plans. As phone therapists, we can take comfort in the knowledge that suicide helplines and crisis lines have long been delivered by phone. One of the oldest, the Samaritans, was established nearly 70 years ago. Before the term disinhibition was coined to describe the client's experience of talking unguardedly in therapy when they can't see their therapist, it was realised that callers to suicide crisis lines retained a sense of control, feeling free to talk and discuss matters they experienced as far too risky to share face to face.

During anxiety-provoking developments, it is always reassuring for phone practitioners to remember that phone therapy has been practised for over 50 years and is an effective medium. We know that disinhibition will allow clients to talk more openly about anguish and despondency about life. Our role is to work collaboratively with clients, helping them to engage positively with risk, holding out for and exploring the potential for change (Reeves, 2015). We know that talking frankly and asking direct questions about suicide do not increase the risk of suicide. This includes ways in which they can look after themselves and draws on personal protective factors such as how they can self-regulate and manage in times of difficulty, connect with safe people and support systems, draw on lessons from previous experiences, participate in activity or exercise. It also means that we signpost the client to additional support for times of crisis outside of session times, researching their local crisis team details and other additional support; see signposting pathways discussed later.

Our responsibility is to bear a client's heartfelt expression of despair while also being courageous enough to talk openly about risk, to ask clear, unambiguous questions to determine their intentions. Various models of assessing suicidal ideation and categorising degrees of risk – low, high and immediate or a traffic light system are widely documented and can help you monitor risk and safeguarding measures. There might be times when it is advisable to obtain guidance on appropriate risk management in relation to certain clients, a client with a formal mental illness diagnosis or mental disorder for instance, perhaps gaining the client's consent to speak to other professionals involved in their care.

Times of crisis can occur rapidly when risk escalates which is why being explicit about the limits of confidentiality in writing and verbally is essential during the assessment process and beyond, when risk occurs. Just like in face-to-face settings, the context of your work will determine your actions and procedures if a client or anyone known to them was in serious, imminent danger of harm. It is likely that you will aim for your client's consent and when this is not possible, you will act with their knowledge but without their permission. Having the client's GP details and emergency contact details to hand is essential. Phone therapy services need clear procedures so that therapists working remotely are not under pressure to act, only to find that although contact details have been collected during the intake process, they don't have immediate access to them.

Managing other types of risk and safeguarding

In addition to the risk of the client harming themselves, there are other circumstances which might escalate into a crisis which involves an external threat to the client.

For instance in cases of domestic abuse, contracting where and when sessions will occur is crucial to collaboratively agreeing to risk management. This might involve discussions about data security covered in Chapter 5. Contracting is likely to include agreement about how necessary contact in between sessions can occur safely and signposting to other sources of support outside of session times. It could also involve terminating the session if their privacy is breached, perhaps agreeing that the client will let you know by using a safe word so that there is no ambiguity between a call ended to keep safe and a technical glitch.

There might be other kinds of risk to the client which raise safeguarding concerns and as part of our role as therapist, we need to balance the therapeutic relationship, client confidentiality and legal and ethical considerations.

As in face-to-face therapy in the UK, safeguarding of our clients involves understanding the legislative and statutory framework and keeping up to date with any changes. In the UK, legislation for children under the age of 18 years is the Children Act (1989) amended by Adoption and Children Act (2004) and legislation to protect vulnerable adults is the Care Act (2014) and Mental Capacity Act (2005). Also, we need to know the types of abuse and neglect for both adults and children (see Chapter 7 for types of child abuse and neglect).

Safeguarding procedures are drawn up within legal frameworks and these can differ in different parts of the UK. Within duty-of-care requirements of organisations if we work for an organisation and within supervision, we contemplate the therapeutic contract and the parameters of confidentiality. We discuss whether we need to report (being clear about whether it is a legal obligation to report, for example Female Genital Mutilation (FGM); or a duty to report as a contractual employment requirement; or as an ethical decision), who we will report to (for example, supervisor, safeguarding lead or local authority), whether this is a breach of the confidentiality contract and how we will record the matter. Moreover, we need to be mindful of how safeguarding and waivers of confidentiality are worded and discussed with client (see Chapter 5, confidentiality).

How you will respond in times of risk, crisis or other safeguarding circumstance needs to be thought through on a case-by-case basis which we continuously monitor, whatever the therapy setting. The BACP's ethical framework for the counselling professions (2018) makes this clear (see Putting clients first, points 9 and 10) and the UKCP provides a five-step approach in their safeguarding guidelines (2018). We assess the seriousness of risk of harm, how imminent the risk is and if we make the decision to disclose to a third party, how effective this will be and how this will impact the client or others as well as the implications if we decide to take action without the consent of the client.

It is best practice to think through and discuss risk and how you will decide to manage this with your supervisor and other colleagues who work on the phone and online. How you act at times of risk will depend on your work setting. If you work for an organisation, then it is likely you will need to inform and consult the designated safeguarding lead as soon as possible. In private practice, this will be talking matters through with your supervisor at the earliest opportunity.

Professional bodies such as the BACP, UKCP, BPS and others have a wealth of information available defining risk, safeguarding and legal obligations across all therapy settings.

The following exercise aims to help you gain clarity regarding risk generally. When we are not physically present with clients, it is wise to talk to your supervisor and/or safeguarding lead or clinical director about risk that could escalate for specific clients in advance of a crisis situation. Exploring a 'what if?' situation could help you to act faster and with certainty if the need arises.

Immediate Risk Management Plan

Consider how you manage immediate risk in a face-to-face setting. What alternative and additional safety procedures need to be put in place?

Think through and discuss with your supervisor and other colleagues who work on the phone and online.

For example:

- Helping vulnerable clients/clients at risk to consider their safety when using the phone, for example last number redial, recent calls, itemised phone bills etc.
- Having client's address, GP details, named person to call in case of emergency on hand
- What additional procedures need to be considered when working with children and young people or vulnerable adults?
- Having an additional phone in your room to make a call while still in phone contact with your client
- Under what circumstance would you call an ambulance, police or fire service?
- Writing a phone therapy service risk management policy which is common knowledge to all therapists. Creating a phone therapy critical risk procedure flow chart which quickly and clearly shows what action to take in different circumstances.
- If the session overruns due to a crisis situation, what will happen regarding your next client?
- How and with whom will you debrief after an emergency or stressful situation?
- How will you access appropriate support when holding and continuously monitoring challenging risk-related issues?

Working with eating disorders and substance abuse on the phone

Julie Hill is a therapist who has significant experience of working with addiction. She has worked with eating disorders and substance misuse charities and in her private practice.

How can therapists work safely with clients presenting with an eating disorder?

Julie: It is possible to work effectively with eating disorders on the phone and the key starting point is to have a comprehensive assessment which includes identifying any risks. A full clinical history to understand the type of disordered eating which could be anorexia nervosa, binge eating, overeating, avoidant restrictive food intake disorder (ARFID) or OSFED (other specified feeding eating disorder). Each group holds a risk.

Anorexia nervosa: restricting can result in low body weight where there might be risk of heart failure, reduction of bone density (osteoporosis), muscle loss and weakness and kidney failure.

Bulimia: regular purging can lead to severe dehydration, electrolyte imbalance, which can lead to heart attack or stroke, also acid reflux, dental problems.

Overeating can lead to diabetes, heart attacks and strokes.

OSFED: this is common in that clients' symptoms do not exactly fit the expected symptoms for specific eating disorders.

The assessment is important to gain clarity about the client's presenting issues around eating and how other issues such as trauma, depression and anxiety manifest within that presentation. Specialist training in eating disorders is advisable. It is important to remember that clients often do not follow an exact presentation as everybody's eating disorder is unique to them.

I can see the importance and need for a thorough assessment. How would a generalist therapist discern an eating disorder from a problem with food or eating as part of a wider presentation? Knowing this could be useful for therapists who might think that if eating issues appear at referral stage then phone therapy will not be possible.

Julie: One of my primary assessment questions is 'What does your eating look like?' I ask what the client eats in a typical day and how food impacts their day. I also ask about fluids and compensatory behaviour such as use of laxatives, diuretics and physical exercise. Other questions include why the client has come today, why now and when the problem started. Frequently, trauma and loss and the need to control accompany eating disorders. Regarding assessing the difference between serious eating disorders and problems with eating or food, asking questions to understand the problem helps to tease this out. Is the client being bullied and is eating a means of gaining some control? Is it about self-esteem, a client doesn't like eating in front of a boyfriend after he made a comment about her weight? Is it a confidence issue which stops a young person eating lunch in front of others but eats normally at home? Is throwing sandwiches away and not eating at school a way of bonding with peers? Working in a psychoeducational way can help the client relate and understand behaviours; so, knowledge of nutrition and eating would be helpful for therapists. It helps to understand the difference between overeating and a binge, an extra serving or a slice of cake is not a binge. It also helps to know the difference between 'physical eating' – knowing I can eat later, I can wait and 'emotional eating' – I see a chocolate wrapper and must have it now. The motivation to eat is different. All of this can form a part of the assessment process.

As a specialist, I imagine your clients are likely to be referred with an eating disorder as a main presenting issue.

Julie: As a counsellor I do not diagnose disorders and my referrals are typically those clients with a mild-to-moderate diagnosis. It is important to have specialist training to recognise when a client would need Tier 3 medical support, as detailed earlier. Whether therapists work face to face, on the phone or video, we work within competence, and this includes getting specialist eating disorder training, particularly, if working with diagnosed disorders.

Whatever the setting, therapists working within their competence is essential. How do you handle risk when you work on the phone?

Julie: The therapy contract is fundamental. If the assessment indicates risk and or, the therapist feels the client needs medical involvement, clients can give permission to form a working alliance with other professionals and myself. Sometimes, we include a nutritionist. Contracting might include permission to contact the client's GP and regular weight monitoring will be agreed with the client or therapy cannot take place. Clients don't need to know their weight; I often arrange a weekly call to the practice, or the GP will email me the current weight. Sometimes, not knowing their weight can be beneficial to the client as we can focus on underlying issues. When working on the phone, video or face to face, building the relationship, congruence and developing trust are very important. We can support clients with recovery, but eating disorders are often entrenched long-standing behaviours. Therefore, risk assess, contract with clients, sometimes including medical professionals and ensure you have relevant information to refer or signpost clients to other services, if required.

Can you give an example of when risk meant that it was inappropriate to work on the phone?

Julie: When the therapist is concerned about the client's physical and emotional well-being, working face to face or video would be safer. Also, when a client is vulnerable and presents with severe mental health issues, which could put them at risk when working with deep-routed issues. However, it is possible to work with eating disorders on the phone and it can be helpful for some clients who are struggling. They can feel more relaxed and less self-conscious. Collaborative work with other professionals such as nutritionists and GP (to monitor weight, bloods for example) can allow therapy to take place within safe parameters and monitor risk. Another important element is for the therapist to have a supervisor who has experience in eating disorders for support and advice.

Some therapists might worry that the client will hide the severity of their eating disorder if they can't be seen but I think that disinhibition can allow clients to seek therapy without shame or embarrassment about how they look. Have you noticed the disinhibition effect when you work on the phone?

Julie: Definitely. For instance, it can be advantageous to work with compulsive eating, emotional eating or binge eating disorder on phone as the client can often feel ashamed and lonely. Society shames overweight people and phone therapy allows clients to open up without fear of judgement. This also works for clients who have low BMIs. My client feedback shows that it is helpful to work via telephone, especially with body image. Clients sometimes request telephone therapy over face to face, which allows them autonomy from the outset. COVID-19 has changed the way we view therapy and given clients' and therapists' choice, it has been beneficial, especially when working with this client group. We have seen positive recovery and good success rates when working on the telephone, where clients with eating disorders can feel relaxed, more comfortable and less judged.

It sounds like phone therapy can be a good medium for eating disorder clients. Can you share any particularly helpful ways of working with this client group on the phone?

Julie: I feel that working creatively is possible on the telephone. Visualisation is one way that can be very helpful when working with phone clients who binge eat. Clients can relax and experience a heightened sense of their therapist's voice and tone, which can be powerful to the exercise. I find working through the stages of the binge can be helpful to the client. First, thinking and planning the binge, then having the food in front of them. The middle stage is eating the food, where clients often dissociate to distract from their feelings. Then the after stage, which allows them to get in touch with difficult emotions after a binge, such as shame and regret. The visualisation can help to give the client insight and a clearer understanding of their binge cycle. This can offer control in how they manage behaviours and subsequent binges in the future.

I imagine that is a powerful visualisation for your clients – helping them to get comfortable first, perhaps lying down, which is easier when they're not being seen, then setting the scene. Visualisation on the phone works really well. As the client is unseen and not self-conscious, they can focus on the therapist's voice without visual distraction.

Thinking about addiction now, when I train therapists, I find that there is a concern about not seeing people who drink or use drugs, that I can't smell the client or see them looking dishevelled.

Julie: There are many similarities with eating disorders and substance misuse and some skill sets are transferable. I would suggest that, as with eating disorders, the therapist gains knowledge around substance misuse when working with this client group. As with eating disorders there are risks which need to be assessed before working with a client. A thorough assessment to ascertain risk is paramount before working with a client. Whether working face to face or the telephone, a contract stating the client refrains from drinking or using substances prior to a session is often implemented (although some people with severe anxiety may use as a way of calming and relaxing prior to a session. This can be addressed in the counselling session). In phone therapy, we listen to detect any substance use such as confusion, muddled speech and slurring of words. This issue can be addressed in the session and the decision to stop the session, if required. As always, the relationship is key to the success of the work, and it is important for the therapist to have a knowledgeable supervisor.

What about risk factors when working with alcohol or drug addiction?

Julie: A thorough assessment is essential. I ask the same question as my eating disorder clients, 'What does your drinking or drug taking look like?' Does the client use during the day, do they hide drink, binge and so on. Assessing risk, particularly with alcohol and heroin, the two physically addictive substances, is important as clients might need additional medical care. They can be very physically unwell should they abstain too soon and medical intervention to titrate the client would be required. With other substances the client can experience uncomfortable physical and emotional feelings and GP support may be required to help the client. Other support and onward referral are important, when required. This will involve researching and signposting to agencies in the client's local area, such as agencies that offer group work and practical support or local 12-step groups.

Referral and signposting pathways

Safeguarding referral and signposting might involve contacting the local authority or other service where the client lives. A search online will provide contact details of national organisations that provide information and support for vulnerable individuals such as children, victims of human trafficking, sexual violence, domestic abuse, migrants, for example.

I introduce the possibility of referral occurring in my therapy contract by stating, 'If I believe that telephone counselling is not suitable for you or proving of benefit to you, I will discuss this with you and support you to access more suitable help'. This paves the way for a discussion about the client's next steps. If the referral is connected to therapist competence rather than the phone setting and the client needs either phone or online therapy, any search you undertake on the client's behalf will need to identify therapists who offer remote working. The advantage in such cases is that the client won't be limited to therapists in their local area.

It can also be useful to suggest other avenues of support to phone clients. This might be because they would like additional information or express an interest in getting in touch with others who experience similar problems. This is particularly helpful for clients who access specialist phone therapy, as is the case for my private practice clients who live apart from their children. I signpost to the charity MATCH www.matchmothers.org.

It is useful to have compiled signposting lists to send to clients when needed. Phone helplines have provided vital listening support, information and advice for decades before online services and are still just as relevant today. You might decide to prepare in advance, lists of helplines, self-help groups, websites, chatrooms, Apps under different categories, for example crisis and suicide support, specialist groupings such as young people, LGBTQIA+, bereavement, domestic abuse, older people, disability groups, carers, sexual abuse and so on. Apart from easy access, prior research will ensure that you signpost clients to services that are secure, effective not harmful – sadly some are, like those encouraging self-harming behaviour. The Helplines Partnership is a useful starting point with over 350 UK and international support organisations.

Blended therapy and the blended assessment

Working with individual clients via a variety of settings – phone, video, text and face to face – is known as blended or hybrid working. The reason why therapists and clients agree to move between settings will vary, as will decisions about which settings work best for the client and the therapist. The decision to work in a blended way might be an organisational one, where choice offered to clients and accessibility are paramount. Private clients and those seen within agencies might request greater flexibility for reasons linked to resources such as time, money and means of travel. In my own practice for example a young person might request blended sessions on a week-by-week basis due to their parent's availability to give them a lift to the therapy room.

A therapist might suggest blended sessions as part of the process of the work, perhaps face-to-face sessions when difficult material arises, such as insecure attachment for example. Likewise, a client and a therapist might agree to phone therapy sessions to allow for exploration of shameful or embarrassing experiences where explicit details of say sexual abuse, dysfunction or addiction can be expressed without having to bear their therapist's gaze.

Wilson and Dunn (2020) suggest a two-assessment model for blended working where ideally, the therapeutic relationship starts with one session face to face and one remotely before agreeing to work together. If two consecutive assessment sessions aren't possible, another assessment is advisable whenever the setting changes.

I think the two-session assessment model is helpful. Wilson and Dunn advocate a collaborative approach to appraise the client's resilience and ability to manage change. Even when the setting is not blended, phone therapy requires a more collaborative approach during assessment, contracting and throughout the work.

Here are some points to bear in mind when offering the combination of phone and face-to-face blended therapy.

- Discuss how the change in setting is experienced by the client, the therapy room or a room in their home, their office, school or other location. Privacy will be an obvious consideration as well as discussion about how the client feels about the phone, other device or room – perhaps how our voice changes in person, whether the phone feels like an intermediary in the process, how it feels to hear other therapists and clients coming and going in the building and so on.
- Encouraging an open discussion about what we might require more of or less of when we can and can't see each other might include anything from managing background noise, more encouragers or shorter silences or session times on the phone.
- Discuss the experience of being able to see each other in the room if therapy has started on the phone. Explore any fantasies or assumptions the client might have about you the therapist for example their age, gender expression, choice of clothes, how the therapy room looks and so on. The therapist might

also share, being mindful of what observations need to be spoken about in supervision rather than discussed with the client.

- Consider how disinhibition experienced by the client during phone sessions will be managed afterwards in a face-to-face setting. For instance, if the client has shared difficult material on the phone that they might not have done if working face to face, they could feel vulnerable or fearful of judgement or rejection. If transference has been experienced strongly, perhaps a client expressing anger towards a therapist, the face-to-face encounter could stimulate shame in the client.

The therapist's experience of blended working is just as relevant. Reflect on the differences both settings represent to you.

- Which feels more secure and private with a client and is this to do with the physical space or the technology or what the client is bringing to the relationship?
- Can you hear the client more easily on the phone or in the room?
- Is it easier to focus and concentrate in one of the settings and do body language cues assist or detract from this?
- How does it feel to be seen and not seen, does this vary between clients?
- On a practical level, how does dressing to been seen by a client, travel time to the room, room hire charges or the physical presence of a client in your home environment make a difference to you and your work with clients?

If you offer blended working, practical matters should discussed, agreed with the client and provided in writing as part of your contract or re-contracting, if blended therapy occurs at a later date. For example:

- Will you be working to an agreed pattern of blended, for example three phone sessions and one face to face or working flexibly from session to session?
- Will the setting for the next session be agreed at the end of the preceding session and any change will require a specific notice period, say 24 or 48 hours or are you willing to accept a last-minute phone session which would otherwise have resulted in a missed session?
- Will there be any changes to how you will handle risk?
- Will the session day and time remain the same?
- Will the session length remain the same?
- Will the session charge remain the same?

Sometimes, how the client experiences transition between different settings takes a few sessions to become evident. I have worked with clients who were keen to work in the room after starting therapy on the phone and for a variety of reasons decided that phone therapy is a better option for them. Monitoring the blended setting, inviting the client to notice changes over time and bringing them to the session to explore them, are all part of collaborative working.

References

BACP. (2018). *BACP ethical framework for the counselling professions.* www.bacp.co.uk/media/3103/bacp-ethical-framework-for-the-counselling-professions-2018.pdf

BACP. (2021). *BACP safeguarding and managing risk.* www.bacp.co.uk/media/8549/bacp-safeguarding-and-managing-risk-3.pdf

BACP Online and Phone Therapy (OPT) competence framework. (2021). www.bacp.co.uk/media/10849/bacp-online-and-phone-therapy-competence-framework-feb21.pdf

Hawkins, P., & Shohet, R. (2012). *Supervision in the helping professions.* Amsterdam University Press.

Reeves, A. (2015). *Working with risk in counselling and psychotherapy.* SAGE.

Reeves, A. (2021). *BACP good practice In action 120 fact sheet: Working with risk within the counselling professions.* BACP. www.bacp.co.uk/media/12848/bacp-working-with-risk-fs-gpia120-sept21.pdf

Suler, J. (2004). The online disinhibition effect. *Cyber Psychology & Behavior, 7*(3), 321–326. https://doi.org/10.1089/1094931041291295

UKCP. (2021). *UKCP guidelines for working online or remotely.* www.psychotherapy.org.uk/media/jrohoner/ukcp-guidelines-for-working-online-or-remotely-v1-0.pdf

Wilson, J., & Dunn, K. (2020). *Two assessment model.* BACP. www.bacp.co.uk/media/11151/bacp-covid-19-blended-approach-member-resource.pdf

Chapter 7

Equality, diversity and inclusion within phone therapy

'Can someone with hearing loss still have phone therapy?'
'What if a client has a disability and doesn't disclose it?'
'How will I notice and talk to a client about their race or culture without visual cues to prompt me?'
What if a client sounds like a man but has a woman's name? How do I open up discussion about sexual identity?'
'What do I need to bear in mind when I work with children, young people and older people on the phone?'

These are some of the questions asked and explored when I train therapists. The UKCP's 'Guidelines for working online/remotely' recognises that 'Geographical distance minimises some of the practical issues of offering therapy and opens-up possibilities for many to work with more diverse clients'. It wisely goes on to caution, 'Cultural differences may be more complex working online/remotely and it can be easier to make presumptions' (2021, 5.3).

The purpose of this chapter is to reflect on key EDI areas through the lens of working with clients on the phone. To do this, I have invited therapists who have a special interest in different aspects of EDI to share their knowledge and experience.

Equality, diversity and inclusion needs to be at the heart of our therapy practice. Equality is about fairness and apportioning equal value and equal worth to all clients, diversity involves respecting a wide range of differences, and inclusion is essential to ensure a broader access and redress power imbalances as much as possible. In the UK, the starting point for assimilating EDI into our practice is the Equality Act (2010), which specifies nine protected characteristics: age; disability; gender reassignment; marriage and civil partnership; pregnancy and maternity; race; religion and belief and sex and sexual orientation. Some of these characteristics are relevant to everyone and some to a smaller demographic.

We live in an increasingly diverse society where there is a growing need to accept our moral and ethical obligation to respect difference. As therapists we aim to inform ourselves and stay open to how unconscious bias impacts our lives and our work.

DOI: 10.4324/9781003253396-7

As therapist Steve Rattray asserts,

> If we as practitioners want to avoid the risk that some aspects of our clients may not be noticed by us, we need to look beyond appearance and physical capacity, beyond gender and cultural backgrounds as the concept of EDI genuinely encompasses all our lives.
>
> (Rattray, 2016)

Disability

Mel Halacre is an integrative counsellor who specialises in disability and trauma and is a member of the BACP EDI task and finish group to support the disability agenda. In 2009, Mel and her husband, who has a spinal cord injury, established the non-profit organisation Spokz People CIC, a mental health service for disabled people and their families. In addition to an online well-being community and psychological programme for clients, Mel has created an online platform for therapists, which provides a range of training and ongoing support via a forum, peer support and supervision.

Mel explained that there is a lack of disability-affirmative therapists in the UK. As therapists are generically trained and there tends to be a belief that unconditional positive regard means that training isn't needed, therapists are often unaware of how working with disabled clients can be different; for example working more flexibly and with blurred boundaries such as doing home visits, although this wouldn't be an issue for phone therapy.

She pointed out that as around 20% of people are disabled, many therapists are already working with disabled clients and said,

> Because disability is the one minority group that any of us can instantaneously belong to, there are a lot of unconscious processes that therapists aren't really aware of. Society tends to focus on the medical approach, the client's impairment, when so much of what disabled people struggle with psychologically is actually around how they get treated by society. In therapy this means that therapists' counter transferential difficulties around disability play an important part.

I understand that accessibility in face-to-face settings can be a real issue for disabled people, that there can be frustrating misunderstandings when therapists tick a box saying they work with disabled people on online listings without thinking through physical accessibility. Does this mean that the phone is a good option for disabled people?

Mel: Yes and no – in my experience it is a good option for some disabled people. Phone therapy can be a great option for disabled people because of pain, travel, mobility or personal care issues. Equally though, isolation can mean that clients prefer an in-person connection. There can be higher levels of mental health issues among the disabled population due to birth or medical trauma, abuse including childhood abuse and attachment issues. Clients with trauma or dissociation might be better able to work on the phone after initially working face to face to build up trust.

I can understand the importance of disability training for therapists, particularly when it comes to assessing suitability. Where phone therapy is appropriate, I would imagine there can be advantages such as client autonomy through use of their own phone, not needing a lift to a therapy room or requiring an assistant to accompany the client.

Mel: For some people, the phone will definitely open doors. Impairments and client circumstances differ hugely. Privacy can be an issue if clients need a lot of support, particularly in care homes. It will be important to check whether the client is using their own phone and whether they are alone. There can be problems with clients in care homes like staff not taking therapy sessions seriously, clients not being ready for sessions or being interrupted. These need to be managed.

Without the frame of the room, therapists need to be aware of the issues and challenges and work with and around them. With so many different impairments, each client needs to be considered individually. Can you highlight important considerations for assessment and contracting with disabled clients?

Mel: It starts with the therapist sharing their experience of disability and their understanding of the social model on their website or listing. So much of disability is lived through the medical model that when clients hear that you understand the social model and feel that you can see the bigger picture, they will know that you see how society treats them. Research shows that what gives people the most mental health difficulties is not their impairment but how they are disabled by society. The language we use is important. Impairment and disability are different. Even though the client might use a particular language and use it interchangeably, we need to show that we understand the difference between medical and social models. To show we understand that disability is the same as race and that there is discrimination, we use the term 'disabled person'. If you say, 'a person with a disability', it shows that you are referring to the medical view. A lot of people don't want to say they are disabled because it is so stigmatised, so they might say, I've got MS, for example.

Disabled clients can suffer assessment fatigue. My family has about 20 different assessments per year. These can be repetitive, traumatic and fatiguing, so anything a therapist can do to reduce that labour is really important. As therapists can be unconsciously activated, they might try and fix or push away. There is also a risk of 'disability spread'; in other words, you see one aspect of the client and it spreads out to all of them and everything presented gets put down to being disabled. Equally unhelpful is the elephant in the room when therapists are too scared to bring the subject up which then silences the client. In my training, I talk about a permission statement in the assessment session – where therapists can acknowledge differences between them and the client and assure them that it's ok to talk about these differences, including disability. Therapists can show that they understand the social model point of view and say something like,

> I recognise that there might have been times in your life when you have been silenced, when you have felt disabled not by your impairment but by society. I'm ok for you to bring that and it's also ok not to.

The literature shows that clients have often felt that their therapist has said that their anger means they haven't accepted their impairment. If you understand the social model, then you will say to your client, 'Your anger is valid, if this happened to me I would feel this anger too and you need to express it'. Therapists can also feel that anger is directed at them personally – if you're a non-disabled therapist it might be. It might feel like it's a personal attack, but it's a projection from the client about the attitude of society on to the non-disabled person.

The permission statement sounds like it can really open up a dialogue. I can also see that in the absence of anything that might indicate your awareness in the room, language and terminology will be important in the phone therapy setting. Would self-disclosure help to show understanding and build trust?

Mel: Most people from minority groups have a kind of sixth sense and are very good at reading other people's non-verbal communication. A client will pick up straight away if you don't have experience of disability. So you may as well self-disclose because the client knows anyway. For example awkward silences are a way that I pick up on this.

An awkward silence is definitely something that phone therapists would want to avoid.

Mel: Self-disclosure, permission statements and if you don't have experience, owning it, possibly decreasing your fee because you are learning on the job will help. There is very little awareness and training, and unfortunately disabled people are used to paying to educate other people.

Not expecting the client to educate the therapist plays a pivotal role in raising awareness around EDI in therapy. Not making assumptions but asking questions is fundamental to phone therapy. Can you say more about asking questions and using self-disclosure when working with disability?

Mel: Communicate a baseline understanding in which you are not looking at disability from a medical model but from a wider view. You are then viewing the client individually and together with your permission statements you're not making assumptions but saying is this something you want to talk about. My approach is to let the client know that I don't necessarily have direct experience, but I am happy to sit alongside them or find out together. When I first encountered a client experiencing pain, I suggested they go to a pain clinic without realising that some services are really inadequate. I think there is a lot more that is asked of us in terms of our personal input and personal disclosure. I use a lot of personal disclosure if a client is isolated and doesn't have a lot of resources to draw on or if they have fewer life experiences. For example if you are discussing sex with a client and they have been sheltered from birth or have been to a special educa-tion school, where sometimes they haven't learned to read and so can't access the internet or other resources, it will be harder to elicit ideas from a client. So we are more holistic and flexible and also incorporate advocacy in our work when needed.

I can see that a flexible approach is beneficial for clients.

Mel: Someone selects an EDI therapist because they know they have experi-ence and they feel isolated and would like that shared experience with their thera-pist, but clients will also pick up on unconscious disclosures around EDI from the therapist.

How would that work on the phone?

Mel: Sometimes, if you've been rejected in your life, you're looking for it and some of that initial reading of eye contact and body language is cut away with the phone, that could be a helpful thing.

Without visual cues, client expression can be unrestrained, they don't have to bear therapist's facial expression. It can be easier to talk about difficult material without being seen, like sex or expressing anger.

Mel: I'm thinking of shame rage, when rage comes from a place of shame and if you don't intervene you risk the client terminating. I would say on the phone, make sure the client isn't going too quickly and that you interject enough.

Absolutely, in absence of body language we need verbal connection, audible nods.

Mel: With disabled or any kind of EDI client issues, those awkward silences are the tell-tale signs of therapist discomfort and avoidance, and so a lack of verbal communication would be even more apparent on the phone. People from minori-tised groups are good at reading those signals, perhaps too soon; so, as therapists we need to be aware of the need for verbal communication so that the client doesn't feel silenced or rejected, particularly around difficult issues. For example sex is taboo, but sex and disability are seen by many in society as an even greater taboo. In the assessment I normalise and include a permission statement saying, 'Here you can talk about sex'.

You mentioned learning disability, what do we need to bear in mind?

Mel: A colleague who works with learning-disabled clients says that it can be harder to start conversations and make connections without non-verbal communication. She says that clients can be very situational, unable to think beyond where they are, in a space without you being visible. Consider mental capacity and risk factors when you assess suitability for phone therapy. You will probably need to work at a slower pace and recap, particularly if there are memory issues. You might also help the client by providing notes at the end of sessions.

Have you any other thoughts about communication and disability on the phone?

Mel: A client's breathing might not be linked to the emotional, it might be as a consequence of their impairment. So it's important to include breathing observa-tions or issues in the assessment. A client might go quiet if they are having a pain flare-up. This might include asking in the early days, 'Are these silences normal for you, or do you want me to ask when this happens?' Don't assume, just ask. Disabled people are used to being asked all the time. With speech impairments, when people are upset their speech may deteriorate and it may be harder to understand them. When one of my clients cries, I can't hear properly, so I say, 'It's ok, I'm here, I can't hear you but we'll get around to it when you're ready'. When she's calmed down a bit, I'll ask her to repeat what she's said. This client has said that previous therapists haven't asked, they pretend they've heard, and she said she feels they're not being authentic.

That is clear and profound feedback from the client. I think you've made a crucial point. You're not always going to hear clearly during phone therapy, maybe an accent or a speech impairment. Being honest and congruent with clients allows for the client to be understood and frees us up. It is possible to find our stride with how individual clients present, relax our way into it and have to ask for a repeat when we need it.

Hearing loss

Phone therapy is often cited as not being possible for clients with hearing loss. I can understand this conjecture, without being able to read lips and body language, it could be easy to assume that voice and hearing alone are not enough. However, not making assumptions is a key element of phone therapy and working with clients who experience hearing loss is no exemption.

According to the Royal National Institute for Deaf People (RNID), hearing loss affects 12 million people in the UK. Hearing loss and deafness happen when sound signals don't reach the brain. There are two main types of hearing loss although it's possible to have both, and this is known as mixed hearing loss. The first type is sensorineural hearing loss, which is caused by damage to the hair cells inside the inner ear or damage to the hearing nerve or both. This makes it more difficult to hear quiet sounds and reduces the quality of sound. Sensorineural hearing loss is permanent but can often be treated with hearing aids. The second type is conductive hearing loss, which can be temporary or permanent depending on the cause. It occurs when the ear loses its ability to transmit sound, for example because of a blockage, such as ear wax or a condition such as otosclerosis where the tiny bones in the ear change shape. Tinnitus is the name for hearing noises that are not caused by an outside source. Around one in eight adults in the UK have tinnitus all the time or regularly. Most cases of tinnitus are linked to hearing loss caused by damage to the inner ear, such as through normal ageing or exposure to loud noise but a third of people with tinnitus have normal hearing, and many people with hearing loss don't have tinnitus.

Judith Sweetman is a person-centred and cognitive behavioural therapist with lived experience of hearing loss and tinnitus caused by otosclerosis. Judith uses hearing aids and I asked her for her thoughts on phone therapy for clients with hearing loss.

I have heard that although hearing loss is the second most common disability in the UK, it is considered an invisible disability as it often goes unnoticed. How can phone therapists ensure they gain an understanding of a hearing-impaired client's needs during sessions?

Judith: There are different categories to hearing loss. If you were born with hearing loss, your experience of life will be different to someone who has had full hearing and then loses it. If you've experienced hearing loss for your whole life, there will be different challenges and issues to if the loss happens later in life, perhaps as part of illness or ageing. If a client has recently experienced hearing loss, that might be a really important issue to bring to therapy, whereas someone who already lives well with hearing loss might not mention it at all. So, what a client needs in terms of hearing impairment will vary – maybe it will be about a big loss but maybe it's more about accessibility initially and not spoken about much after the initial discussion.

Asking pertinent questions during the assessment sounds important. How would you go about this?

Judith: The key thing is to ask, not assume. I wouldn't even use the term hearing loss. During the assessment, as a starting point for exploring clients' needs and accessibility, I would ask the client a broad, open question like, 'Is there anything I should be aware of that might affect our conversation? For example, some people find it hard to hear, some people find it difficult to talk on the phone, for others it might be about technical issues'.

So it sounds like you would wait for the client to tell you about hearing loss and use the language they use to describe it. Do therapists need to consider how they speak – their pitch or volume?

Judith: I would say be led by initial open conversation – you don't want to be patronising. In my case, I have hearing loss, but I can hear you absolutely fine on the phone; but phone therapy might be difficult for clients with a hearing impairment for reasons other than mine. At the beginning stage of therapy via the phone, some people might find the phone tiring whether or not they are hearing impaired. They might lose focus or miss something. I would let the client know that if they ever want me to repeat something that's fine, just let me know. I might ask whether there was anything I can do to help them access phone therapy more fully, but I wouldn't change the way I spoke. Saying that, sometimes I find softly spoken people with accents more difficult to hear. If that was the case with my therapist, I would want them to be patient and acknowledge it. It would be helpful if they said, 'Sometimes people find my accent difficult. Please let me know if you need me to speak up'.

I like that. Therapists with accents on my training courses sometimes worry about being understood by all their clients, never mind those with hearing loss, so naming it as you have just suggested might be useful.

Judith: Another way could be to frame it from yourself, 'Sometimes I find that working on the phone can feel more intense because I have to concentrate to really listen properly, is that something you ever experience?' Remember, the client might not perceive themselves as someone with a disability. Maybe they consider their hearing loss like loss of sight; your vision might be impaired to the extent that you need to be wearing lenses or glasses to drive but you might not consider this a disability because the glasses or lenses correct the problem.

Avoiding assumptions, noticing how the client identifies as hearing impaired is important. What about adaptations and equipment considerations for phone therapy?

Judith: There are two parts to adaptation. The first is that the person adapts to the hearing loss on a personal level. Then there are technical adaptations such as hearing aids. Most of the time I don't need you to adjust how you speak because my hearing aids work really well.

I know that hearing aids and phone technology can make a real difference and there are developments all the time; what is your experience of this?

Judith: Mobile phone calls get streamed to my hearing aids via Bluetooth. My hearing aids work like earbuds, I usually get incredibly good hearing from my mobile phone as the sound is streamed directly into my ears. Personally, I struggle to hear my landline because of the way handsets are designed, they are often not very compatible with behind-the-ear hearing aids. When I'm on a landline call, I use loudspeaker, so privacy would need to be discussed if I were a phone therapy client. Another thing to be aware of is that hearing aid power runs out in the same way as when we lose power in our phones.

A therapist wouldn't be talking to client about charging hearing aid would they, that could be really condescending?

Judith: I agree, but knowing it can occur is useful. I charge my hearing aids every night, and the power generally lasts all day unless I do a lot of streaming. My previous hearing aids were battery-powered and I would occasionally have to pause to change the battery when they run down. As therapists, we want clients to share as much as they want and to be comfortable. We can give them the space for this in assessment by saying things like, 'Ah ok, tell me what's that like. . .. tell me more about that . . . I wonder what that's like for you?'

I imagine therapists would think that advising a client to use a headset would take care of them being overheard by others.

Judith: The general advice given for online and phone therapy is to use a head-set, but they can be a nightmare. As my hearing aids sit behind my ear, standard headsets don't work for me. I use conductive headphones instead, which are bril-liant as they bypass the part of my ear that doesn't work properly, but they can be less confidential than standard headphones because some sound escapes from them. Most often though, I use Bluetooth to stream directly to my hearing aids which is like using earbuds.

I can see the essential starting point is not to assume that if your client has hearing loss, the phone won't be an appropriate medium. It's really important to see your client as an individual without judgement or bias focus and focus on understanding their world.

Judith: It's about checking, asking clients what they need. I think the phone is a great medium for therapy. As you aren't looking at each other or basing your understanding on what you can see, it can be very allowing and destigmatising. As a client or as a therapist, the phone can actually be easier for me because the technology, particularly Bluetooth, minimises interference. I can focus my energy on listening and hearing without having to watch lips for extra cues when a lorry rumbles past the window for example or miss something when someone turns their head away.

Race and culture

Anthea Benjamin is a UKCP-registered integrative arts psychotherapist, adolescent therapeutic counsellor, group analyst and supervisor. She works as a therapist delivering training and running groups for couples at the Tavistock Centre for Couple Relationships and also has a London-based private practice.

Jessie Emilion is a cognitive analytic psychotherapist, supervisor and trainer, member of UKCP EDI taskforce, BACP EDI task and finish group. She is the cognitive analytic psychotherapy lead in Southwark, South London and Maudsley NHS Foundation Trust.

Without being able to see a client, what are your views on when and how to ask about race and culture? How can phone therapists avoid being colour blind?

Anthea: When I'm training therapists I talk about opening things up in a general way, exploring people's differences, what is their family background, the social and political context they grew up in and was there any experience of discrimination or marginalisation. That way we aren't having to say – are you black or Asian – we are keeping a general awareness around how these social experiences are absolutely key in forming someone's sense of self, sense of safety, being in relationships and attachment triggers. There are different ideas regarding practitioners addressing it and some say it's really important to explore people's cultural or racial identity from the beginning. It depends on the individual; some people are really open about doing that. My experience is that sometimes people feel it's a bit jarring to bring up race right at the beginning when they haven't even got a relationship in place. If someone has had a traumatised, racialised experience, they are not necessarily going to want to talk about that from the get-go because of issues around trust, containment and safety.

Jessie: I get asked this often in my training, 'Do we raise race and ethnicity and when and how do we raise it?' Even if you don't see the person the concept is often present in the narrative, it is about active listening and if you are open to the idea of difference in your own mind, you will hear it.

It's important for the therapist to own their positions of power, privilege, where they sit within the hierarchical structure of the society and what they bring into the therapy room both as a person and in transference. The idea of difference be it race, language, religion or culture is often implicitly or explicitly present in the narrative. If it's present in the narrative, then it's important to recognise that the client is communicating something to you and it's often okay to name or address this in the work. Timing is important.

We as therapists should be actively listening in the session, attend to these powerful concepts/constructs in an appropriate and timely manner. It's important for the therapist to be open, honest and engage with the race, language, culture or religion in a non-defensive manner. Recognising our positions of power or disempowerment, feelings of guilt or shame is crucial to this process.

When the session is on the telephone or online, listening to dialects and accents becomes a crucial part of the process of naming the difference. The history and background information of the client may also reveal aspects of identity and lived experiences.

Some clients may prefer male, female, LGBTQIA+, BAME therapists. When working online, it's easy to get into a dilemma of whether we disclose or remain a blank screen. My view on this is not so black and white, but it's more about understanding why this question is important for our client, the meaning behind the question needs to be explored. It's often about arriving at a middle ground where power imbalance in the relationship is discussed. Sometimes, self-disclosure is helpful, similar to when therapy is conducted in person. By withholding information, we may be unconsciously replaying power dynamics within the therapeutic relationship.

There is so much self-disclosure when we meet our clients in person. Our race, the way we dress, where we meet our client, our consulting rooms all reveal aspects of our identity. On the telephone, they can go only by our tone, accent, voice and hence questions around our race or culture become quite central for our clients in connecting with us or having a sense of who we are as a person.

Phone therapy requires that we watch our mind's eye and to avoid making assumptions. We ask more questions, but I think there can be anxiety about asking, fear of saying the wrong thing and causing offence which is where colour blindness occurs. I wonder how we can find the middle ground.

Jessie: Some therapists feel that if we have to ask a client about race, we are boxing them into a category, or it becomes a tickbox exercise. I hold the view that if we don't ask these questions, we are more likely to missing a big part of our client's history or identity and lived experiences. So, we do need to have these conversations, ask the questions without fear which is better than making assumptions and getting the wrong sense of our clients.

Tentative queries, not merely stating our intuitions as facts, are central to this work. We can start by asking – tell me about yourself, who you are, what your life is like and that should give us an idea about our client's experiences and history. Whether you work face to face or on the phone you shouldn't be frightened to ask something like, 'From what you're describing I get the sense that you grew up in this community, am I right in thinking that?' Sensitivity and attunement are important whether it's telephone or in-person counselling.

Anthea: The client might need more of a sense of bedding into the relationship first before talking about race and culture. When they are ready, one of the ideas I like is a concept that has come from family therapy, particularly in the United

States, which they call location of self in the therapy, which brings intersectional identities into the relationship. For example

> I want to let you know that I am white middle class, working class back-ground, but middle-class woman and therefore I am going to have a certain kind of framework of how I see the world. I am actively working on address-ing my own normative, privileged lenses of seeing the world, but I am also aware that there may be thing that I might not spot. I'm not sure how you would locate yourself in terms of intersectionality but I want to name that, I'll be thinking about it but if there is anything that comes up that you feel has been missed in some way, or that your identity hasn't been held in mind, or if there has been anything that's felt offensive, I want you to know that I am very open to you raising it and us thinking about it and addressing that and doing any repair that might be required as a result of that.

On the phone, a more collaborative approach is helpful. I can see how this way of working can be a good fit with EDI and when bearing intersectionality in mind. Without sight of the therapist or visual cues in the room to indicate awareness of EDI, verbal location of self can be useful.

Anthea: It gives permission to talk about power. Even when I'm working face to face and there is a difference, say same-sex couples, I will be naming it immediately,

> I may unconsciously express something around my heteronormative condi-tioning. I am going to be conscious of that, but you might spot something and if it happens, let me know because I don't want to do anything that's going to cause harm or make you feel uncomfortable or in any way makes you feel like you can't bring all of yourself here because this is for you, it's not about my limitations.

It really opens things up, it's easier. I work in adoption and was once talking about attachment cycle, and I referred to 'mother'. That was a trigger for the client, and I thought you're right, that's a very heteronormative way of thinking about it. I thanked them for letting me know, responded non-defensively and repaired it. It deepens the work rather than it becoming that I am the ignorant therapist. If you can work with the vulnerability of that, it can really be helpful.

Without being at therapy room, there can be increased equality, the power dynamics can be more equalised, especially if the client is in their own home in a private space. Together with the disinhibition effect, clients can experience greater freedom to express themselves.

Jessie: Confidentiality and space need to be carefully considered. In some com-munities (BAME or otherwise), there isn't a private space in the house. Therapists need to discuss where the client will be for their session in the car, or will they be walking outside or in a café, for instance. The idea of having therapy is not widely accepted in some marginalised communities. In the NHS and healthcare settings, for example there is a lot of discussion about toxic interaction, inequality and circles of fear that are present between statutory services and BAME communities and the impact of these on access to therapy, engagement and client satisfaction.

With the recent pandemic, most of us have taken to online or telephone work. Some patients have found the distance (not being in the same room as the therapist) helpful in being able to engage with difficult process whilst others have struggled with not having the space or the time to walk from a venue to home, to separate the session from their home life. For most, it has been easier to access therapy online, but we also have clients who don't have the facility or access to equipment, data etc. These are EDI-related issues around class and economy.

On the phone, some clients might be more open to disclosing because they can't see the other person's reaction. Anger or feelings of sadness can be attended to if the therapist is attuned to the client's tone of voice, these can be tentatively checked out.

Where therapy is conducted, especially if there is no therapy room, is a complex area. Issues around the therapeutic frame, how we set up the virtual room space, create a virtual container with boundaries are not straightforward and they are very much about power and trust. Historical betrayal and abuse of power may need to be considered when working with some marginalised communities.

The phone can be liberating for clients sharing difficult material. They don't have to bear the therapist's gaze. What are your thoughts about the experience of not being seen in relation to race and culture?

Jessie: Yes, but sometimes in the BAME community clients do need to see compassion or a positive gaze reflected back to them, something they may not have experienced in their life. In some cultures, direct eye contact with seniors, elders or authority is considered disrespectful or even dangerous. We are focusing on our clients, but I can't help wondering about therapists who don't like seeing their own image on the screen, what is being avoided? If one is not seen in relation to our race or culture, then one is missing a big part of one's identity in therapy. Race and culture are powerful constructs that shape our identity and personality.

Anthea: In terms of culture and difference, experiences have often been through the intense gaze of something happening and not necessarily having a way of communicating it. With racism or any prejudicial or oppressive practice, the essence of that is something awful is happening to me and I don't know how to put that into words, I don't know what to say.

The gaze in the room can feel persecutory and oppressive, so there is something about phone therapy that frees people up. This was true to when I was working with clients who had experienced rape. Working face to face was unbearable for some because of the shame and their level of dysregulation. Just being with someone looking at them even with benign care still felt incredibly unsafe. This relates to people who feel so marginalised that the shame of someone looking at them is overwhelming; so the phone gives them a space. Clients may not need to be in the room, the idea of being in the room better needs to be challenged because you need to meet people where they are at. Also, there are cultures where eye contact and face-to-face stuff just don't feel right, feels really alien, intrusive not comfortable, not a good fit.

Client disinhibition might also be about an expression of anger, a therapist saying something that triggers a response or taps into a vein of anger, say about discrimination.

Anthea: I think it is useful when acting out happens. In a way, it is stuff we wouldn't necessarily get in the room. It's what we do with it that matters, how we make sense of it with the client, how we might be making judgements about what is 'appropriate' around how to be in therapy. It's about what we might regard as outside of the framework and how we think about that without becoming oppressive, judgemental, without power communication towards someone bringing more of their dysregulated parts of themselves into the therapeutic space. It's true to with race and culture and marginalisation. Sometimes, I find myself thinking 'Why did I say that, I know better than that'. You get pulled into replaying something from the field or reacting from your anxiety and there may be the need for repair if it's created a rupture but it's about continuing to think about what this means. One of the difficulties with race is that people too often collapse into shame, not that shame isn't an important part of the process but if therapists don't go beyond that, that's a problem. If you're not able to process it and integrate what has happened, if there isn't enough robustness for staying with it, most of us want to go into flight reaction and get out of there because it's so painful.

That makes sense to me, I know I have to be mindful of not collapsing into shame around race and discrimination. I'm still learning about myself in relation to EDI, it's an ongoing work. I'm also thinking that clients can slip into shame after expressing anger on the phone, the pain of that.

Anthea: I think we need to consider how to invite people into therapy, for most people it's an alien way of being and thinking, and we have to keep checking in, helping people understand how to do this. For some people, silences are very punitive, the work might be to understand where that comes from and expanding their tolerance. For others it may be a cultural thing, everything is alien to them. The question then is about power. Are we going to expect them to do it the way we think we should do it or to find a middle ground which enables the client to do the work they need? Maybe we need to stretch to build that safety and containment and collaborative process.

Jessie: The key thing is not to be worried about getting it wrong and hence avoiding the topic. If it's avoided, it becomes the elephant in the room. If you thoughtfully talk about difference, be it race and/or culture, then there is a chance to have that dialogue on the phone or face to face. You can arrive at some shared understanding or learning. The work is ongoing. Compassion to self and others, humility and willingness to learn are needed for this work so that we can avoid getting into reciprocal roles of shaming to shamed in relationship.

Gender, sexual and relationship diversity (GSRD)

Karen Pollock is an integrative psychotherapist, supervisor and trainer who specialises in GSRD therapy. She is an advanced, accredited gender, sex and relationship diversities therapist as awarded by Pink Therapy and has a busy GSRD practice which includes queer, kinky, non-monogamy as well as LGBTQ+ clients.

On the phone, a client can't be seen, and it might be easier to miss or avoid obvious cues about their GSRD identity. Do you think a therapist should ask about GSRD part of the assessment or should this be left to the client to disclose as it might not be relevant to the presenting issue?

Karen: I am a person-centred therapist and during the assessment I always ask the client their pronouns. I think there are lots of different ways of doing an assessment; some therapists might want quite a lot of information about the client, but I would say two things. Make sure what you ask is necessary and whatever you ask, make sure you ask all clients. If we don't, we are making assumptions about someone we might think is queer or trans and we are othering the client before we even start the process.

You raise an important point about not making assumptions which is even more significant when we don't have visual cues. Can you elaborate a bit more on assumptions and GSRD?

Karen: On the phone, there is the power of not being seen, a liberation to that. When there are a lack of visual cues and we're working with the LGBTQ+ community, unpicking our assumptions has to come front and centre. If not, our stuff will get in the way. Everybody brings social, cultural, familial – the myriad of inputs from birth into how they view other people, that can't be changed but our awareness of this can be raised. We need to do the work ourselves. If somebody says they are asexual and we don't really know what they mean, we make assumptions, it's our stuff getting in the way. In some respects, this is quite basic but it's at the heart of GSRD work. It is liberating for us if we accept that we will make assumptions. Some cues will be obvious, but some won't be. I think that phone therapy could be a real liberation for therapists to think – what if I offer *every* client, not just the one with blue hair and piercings or the person whose gender presentation might not match their name, that blank slate? This makes space for intersectionality. Someone might sound middle class now but maybe they were brought up in poverty. Without imposing our assumptions, we give the client space.

As there is no therapy room to display visual signals of GSRD awareness – pictures, books, flags for instance, how can we normalise and encourage clients to explore GSRD material?

Karen: How can we simply and without being intrusive indicate that we are affirmative or an ally? On my intake form, I ask pronouns. This could be asked in a first session along with therapists offering their own as well. This can work well in phone therapy, it's such a simple act from which the client can gauge that this person at least knows a little bit. For trans clients in particular, the phone can be tricky. They have to live with people hearing their voice, knowing what their name is but insisting that they are not the person they are saying they are, even suspecting them as being fraudulent. So, they have to out themselves as trans to be heard and believed, when they are just trying to make a bank transfer, for example. On phone, we need to unpick our assumptions of what a man, woman, non-binary client sounds like. A handy way to remind yourself by thinking for example, 'This is David Jones, he has high pitched voice, many people might think he has a woman's voice but he has told me his pronouns are he/him, so I'll conceive of him as a man'. Then the client doesn't have to tell you their history because you are doing work, not making assumptions. After all David Jones might be coming for therapy to explore bereavement and being trans is irrelevant.

You've raised an important point; we notice our assumptions so that we can create a space to work with what is relevant for the client.

Karen: How can we let the client know it's safe on the phone? Often, we do this by the words we choose. If for instance we use the word partner, we show that we are aware that partners are not necessarily a certain gender. Likewise, not assuming that only certain types of people have the menopause or that everyone has the same menopause. Just with our words, how we respond shows that we are aware that there's not only one way of doing things or being in relationships. In my experience, it is the clumsy attempts to meet the client that can do harm. It's very rare that therapists are overtly trans/homo/queer phobic these days. It's more the clumsy attempts to meet the client when we haven't done the work to dig into our assumptions and prejudices that are problematic. Imagine two lesbians coming for therapy and one is thinking about transitioning to a non-binary identity. The therapist meets them clumsily by saying, 'I've heard about lesbian bed death, is this a reaction about having less sex?' The therapist wanted to meet them, but the clients are now thinking, 'I didn't mention my sex life, just because you've got this tiny nugget of information, why on earth have you mentioned sex!' This is an example of clumsiness – the therapist not using inclusive and expansive words which allows the client to take us where they need to go.

So inclusive words are powerful, allowing is important and the starting point is for us to educate ourselves.

Yes, so many GSRD clients say they resent it. They are paying us. They don't want to take their time having to explain an aspect of themselves before they can get to the meat – the therapist on the starter of a meal and the client wants to be in the main course. The therapist wants to build the relationship but because they haven't educated themselves, they get sidetracked by GSRD identity. The only exception is if someone comes and presenting issue "I might be", then the main course is the identity, and we do the opposite. The therapist might know loads about what it means to be an aromantic, pansexual demigirl, but that is irrelevant right now. The focus is, what does this mean for the client, what will be the impact of them coming out. Generally, if a GSRD client comes to us about other issues, it's about educating ourselves, looking at our own assumptions and own gender and sexuality. If a client is doing deep dive into exploring identity, without training, consider referring them on. You can't be also learning alongside them. If it's messy for them, it can't be messy for you too.

In what ways do you think the positive (benign) and negative (toxic) disinhibition effect plays out in GSRD phone therapy?

Karen: LGBTQ+ people get sexualised, we sexualise queer bodies and queer identities, we load them with shame. It's the pornographication of being LGBTQ+ and I can see that not being seen in phone therapy, particularly for people still carrying that shame and internalised homophobia, could be really useful because they aren't separate from society.

One of the areas phone therapy could be different is voice dysphoria or dysphoria about any part of body and gendered part of their identity. Many trans people struggle with their voice and will undergo voice coaching. It is easier for transmen because testosterone thickens the vocal cords, but for transfemme, voice can be a source of distress. I don't think that will preclude phone therapy because looking at it compassionately and clearly in the eye is the way we resolve the distress. Dysphoria isn't something we cure, we learn to accommodate, it's not disease to be fixed which is an impact of being trans for some people. Knowing it can be an issue I would raise it as part of the assessment in first session. I'd ask, 'How are you with your voice?', 'How do you feel about me not being able to see you, or see the visual cues that would tell me about your gender, that perhaps you've put a lot of time and effort into making sure are there?' Also, 'Let's explore how it is to only be a voice right now'. Maybe it would be totally liberating for clients without voice dysphoria, perhaps they've had voice coaching or tracheal shave. They might say, 'My voice is totally the way I want to world to see me, it's the other stuff that I'm not quite so happy about'.

Have you any thoughts on disinhibited expression of anger on the phone?

Karen: It is even more important if you are not GSRD yourself, to have unpicked work around your own privileges, own complicity in the society in which many queer people face terrible experiences. That anger needs to come out and therapists need to be able to hear, for example 'Fucking cis people/the straights have screwed up my life/I can't stand that person, fucking breeder'. You might want to be defensive, but let them feel it and they need to express it so as to heal from whatever caused the anger. And that means therapists need to have done the work reflecting on 'What privileges do I have that this trans or bi person doesn't have?' and What might I have said and done in past?' as there might be guilt about this. Be honest about how you've played along, not understood it or laughed at something. Ten years ago, you might have thought transgender people had a mental illness that could be fixed, but now you know this is a different way of being. You've got to be really honest with yourself because if the anger of a client needs to come out you can't squash it down. Let them rant, then afterwards say something like, 'Your mum really hurt you when she called you a pervert and I can hear the anger'.

One of the advantages of phone therapy is that clients can feel more able to bring shame-laden or embarrassing material to sessions because of not being seen.

Karen: Yes, it can be easier for clients talking about sex when they don't have to see the therapist's face if they disclose they went to an orgy at the weekend or like dressing up as a milkmaid. I think because of cultural experience of judgement, it is imperative for the therapist to verbally affirm that they aren't shocked or judging that this is all part of the wonderful experience of being human. If they can't see the therapist's face to see they aren't shocked, recoiling or disgusted, they need verbal affirmation, 'Ok, so you say you had sex with a number of men last night, how do you feel about that?' On the phone, verbally showing lack of judgement is important so they can get past the shame.

Verbally communicating non-judgement is fundamental, audible nods are crucial, and managing silences appropriately is essential.

Karen: So many GSRD people experience rejection by family and friends. I can see that silence is necessary, but therapists have to learn how to use silence on the phone. Rejection is a huge part of queer experience, part of the cultural heritage, so silence needs to be open and welcoming, not silent rejection.

Older people

Care for the Carers is a charity that has been supporting and representing unpaid carers in East Sussex since 1989. Care for the Carers' Time to Talk counselling service is accredited by BACP and offers free counselling to support carers to cope with the emotional impact of their caring role. I asked counsellor and supervisor Siwan Leach, who is the counselling coordinator of Care for the Carers to share her knowledge and experience of offering phone therapy to older clients.

What are the barriers to older people accessing therapy?

Siwan: Many older clients are from a generation when counselling was not widely available and may have been considered unnecessary or a luxury for the elite few. There may also be shame attached to the notion of needing emotional support.

Perhaps not being seen by their therapist helps older clients talk more easily about their problems. In your experience, what are the advantages of offering phone therapy to your clients?

Siwan: There is a huge benefit to offering telephone counselling to older clients, as it provides flexibility for clients who may have difficulty accessing face-to-face sessions for a variety of reasons:

- Mobility issues – housebound clients are able to access telephone services.
- Health reasons – clients who are worried about picking up infections post-COVID can safely access therapy.

- Weather issues – clients do not need to brave winter weather to get to their sessions, so may not lose motivation to attend.
- Financial issues – clients do not need to factor in the cost of transport to and from sessions.
- Time management – clients do not need to factor in travel time, and this is an advantage for carers who may need to minimise time away from home and their caring responsibilities.

What would you regard as being the potential limitations of phone therapy for older people?

Siwan: There can be privacy issues. Older clients are often unaware of the importance of having a quiet, private space free from interruptions and distractions. This may be particularly difficult if the client is a carer at home of a spouse or partner with dementia, for example. Some older clients may also have hearing or speech impairment or a cognitive impairment, and this can have a detrimental effect on the establishment of a therapeutic alliance.

Are there any particular considerations for contracting with your clients?

Siwan: Clients who have not previously accessed counselling may be unaware of the process, so contracting is particularly important. Many older clients may view the sessions as befriending or an optional social 'drop-in' session and may not realise the commitment required to facilitate the best therapeutic outcomes. This commitment can also be affected by external factors such as medical appointments, so explaining the significance of making a time and a space for sessions is part of contracting with our clients. Our contract states the number of sessions we are able to provide as well as the length and frequency of sessions. We discuss cancellation of sessions and non-attendance with clients, that without prior notice, a missed session will be deducted from the total number of sessions, although there is some flexibility to accommodate genuine emergencies, which often happen for carers. Our counsellors moreover explain confidentiality to clients and the limits to confidentiality.

What about your assessment process?

Siwan: It is important to establish the older client's expectations of telephone counselling and in particular to address what it can offer and what it does not! Many older clients who are requesting counselling may in fact be seeking practical support, advice and guidance, and it is prudent to refer clients to other services and organisations which can support them. In this way, the counsellor is free to focus on the therapeutic work rather than to be a 'support worker'. Care for the Carers has a robust assessment process, which in addition to the presenting issues includes the client's GP details, psychological treatment within the last 12 months, any other agencies involved, prescribed medication, support system, any mobility needs, the cared-for person's health issues and a checklist of identified concerns. Also, we have clear guidance for our counsellors on suitability, including psychological suitability, as well as information on risk indicators, assessing risk and safeguarding procedures.

Children and young people

During the COVID-19 pandemic, many of the professional therapy bodies issued guidance for working online and over the phone with children and young people (CYP), for example the UKCP, ACP (Association for child psychotherapists) and the BPS (British Psychological Society) in the UK. At the time of writing, this information was still available online and provides useful advice and recommendations.

Regarding the dearth of training for working online or on the phone with CYP before the COVID lockdown, the UKCP (2021) commented,

> To date none of the UKCP accredited courses have included the development of these skills as part of the training process and therapists need to balance their concern for vulnerable child clients with the ethical imperative of working within the bounds of their professional competence.

Post COVID, the BACP has updated their CYP (4–18 years) competence framework to include competences for online and phone therapy (OPT).

After the hasty transition to remote working, professional training for working with CYP remotely will no doubt follow the move to mainstream online and phone therapy and regard it as a setting rather than a specialism.

The starting point for working with CYP on the phone is to work within the CYP face to face competence framework and guidance of your professional body. This will include requiring knowledge of CYP development, mental health problems, legal frameworks, capacity, informed consent; awareness of EDI – difference within families, for example culture, race, and GSRD and the ability to conduct assessments, communicate with CYP of different ages and developmental stages; develop a working alliance and so on.

In conjunction with the content of the other chapters in this book, the following section includes the considerations contracted therapy sessions with CYP. My own experience does not extend to working with clients under the age of 13 years on the phone; so additional factors relevant to younger children might not be included here and should be sought elsewhere.

Contracting

The following are considerations in addition to generic contracting covered in Chapter 5. Depending on the context, age and capacity of the CYP, the contract might include the parent or carer, and in some cases, the contract and ongoing contact with parent, carer or a third party are an intrinsic part the working alliance. It might also be necessary to verify identity of client, particularly asking for proof of their age. For safety as well as clarity, keep a written record of agreements and consent. The main security issues in the provision of phone therapy, for example recording a phone call, should be clarified and where relevant, online safety discussed.

Confidentiality and the potential threat to confidentially should be clearly established especially regarding the phone itself. Who manages the phone contract, who owns the personal data? Does the CYP client have complete control over the phone they use, is it their own or does it belong to a parent or carer? How accessible is the phone to others, is it possible for others to record or view a text communication between you and your client? Is the phone always with the client or is it sometimes in the care of or shared with others? Could it be confiscated as a punishment? These matters extend beyond security and confidentiality as they could impact on the client's ability to attend a session.

Boundaries and the therapeutic space

As when working with adults, check that you are talking to the client, particularly the first session when a parent or carer might make or receive the call. If this occurs in my practice, after we have greeted each other, I use the opportunity to talk about the client's need for privacy with the adult before discussing it with the client afterwards.

I ask the client where they are, whether they are alone or now alone if an adult was with them at the beginning of the session. I ask how they view their level of privacy and if they express a difficulty with this and or if I sense privacy could be compromised, I initiate a conversation about how they might better achieve this for themselves. This might be about not using speakerphone, putting a music making device by the door, sitting in a particular area of the room, creating make-shift sound-proof 'nest' or having sessions in another location (see Chapter 5 for further details on privacy). We also discuss how we will manage any breaches of privacy, which can be startling for both of us and upsetting for the client.

> Having transitioned a young person client from face-to-face sessions to the phone therapy during the COVID-19 pandemic lockdown, my client's sibling barged into her bedroom during a session and saw her crying. When she was alone once more, my client became very distressed by the intrusion. She was angry that her sibling and her parents (because they had not kept an eye on their other child) had not respected her request for privacy during her appointment with me. She was also worried about how her sibling would react to seeing her upset. We used the rest of the session to explore her experience of the privacy breach, particularly her mixed feelings of anger and wanting to protect her sibling from seeing her cry. The needs of her sibling being regarded as more important than her own within the family had been a common theme in the work during face-to-face sessions. Considering the depth of my client's anguish, I was surprised by her upbeat tone when she called for her next session. She said that as she had initially feared, her bewildered sibling had told her parents about her rarely witnessed upset

which led to a family discussion. Initially alarmed by this, my client said that she discovered that it was possible for her to share her feelings and that she had felt listened to. Thereafter, she reflected on how the privacy breach resulted in her taking a risk and being heard and it also served as a 'wake up call' to her parents about her needs and feelings.

Privacy breaches can provide therapists with direct information about the client's daily experience within their family and home life. As our sense of hearing is heightened during phone therapy, an interruption can reach our senses viscerally.

Another client described struggling with uncaring, angry, controlling parents who showed her scant respect. On one occasion, after a knock on the door which was only just audible to me, I could hear a softly spoken parent ask the client a question. Why this interruption occurred during the session is food for thought but what struck me was the client's response – a loud, vitriolic barrage of retort before I heard a hasty closing of the door as the parent retreated. In an instant with an activated startle response after their loud and angry outburst, I was introduced to a part of the client I had not encountered until that point.

Not all clients will present this way of course and a useful way to manage interruptions is for there to be a discussion about managing privacy which might include agreeing to an 'alert word' or turn of phrase that the client can say to let you know that they are no longer alone and or that they need or would prefer to end the call. Even if the client doesn't mention an intrusion, I will ask about background noise that I think might disturb us.

I prefer to check in and manage the boundaries around the therapeutic space at the beginning of each session by asking the client where they are, whether they feel they are in a private-enough space, with some clients whether anyone else is in the house, whether they need to redial if the line isn't clear enough, whether they are comfortable and so on. This forms the basis of the client's arrival and settling themselves down in our virtual therapy room.

Assessment

The UKCP guidelines for working remotely (2021) state that adjustments to assessments should consider the CYP's 'age, developmental stage, neurodiversity, emotional and behavioural challenges, attention span, environment, timings, parental responsibilities and the overall health and safety considerations of the context'. Being mindful of the need to build a relationship as rapidly as possible without visual cues, and having a flexible approach to accommodate these factors, is important. A detailed information about the need for a robust phone assessment can be found in Chapter 6, but without being able to see each other or any creative material in the therapy room, a relaxed conversational approach can be helpful for CYP, particularly for those who are not very communicative. Having some structure which includes curiosity questions about the client's likes and dislikes, hobbies and interests, what they do for fun with family, whether they have any pets can go a long way to getting to know them and putting them at their ease. The assessment is usually the time to notice and begin talking about EDI considerations, disability, race, GSRD, intersectionality including possible digital poverty if this becomes evident all of which is discussed in Chapter 7. Likewise, assessing and contracting around creative interventions, discussed in Chapter 8, are especially important when working with CYP and might need parents' involvement.

Safeguarding, assessing and managing risk

The most pertinent areas to consider when we work with CYP begin with the need to be aware of legislation and statutory guidance which protects children. In the UK, legislation for children under the age of 18 years is the Children Act (1989) amended by Adoption and Children Act (2004). Also, we also need to be aware of the categories of harm identified within child safeguarding: physical, sexual and emotional abuse and neglect within the home and contextual abuse, namely criminal exploitation, child sexual exploitation, trafficking/modern slavery and online abuse outside of the home.

Assessing safeguarding issues and managing risk can be more difficult when we work remotely with CYP. It requires that we are aware of our role as therapist, the balance between client confidentiality and legal and ethical considerations. Also, we need to be mindful of how safeguarding and waivers of confidentiality are worded and discussed with client. Managing risk is a continuous process and talking through our decisions, seeking advice and support, recording risk and our decisions are essential when we work with CYP.

The Immediate Risk Management Plan prompts in Chapter 6 can help form the starting point for managing risk when working with CYP. The following might contribute to this process:

- Agree session times when your safeguarding lead or other professionals can be contacted straight away.
- Have the contact details of parents and carers immediately to hand along with an additional phone so that you can keep the client on the line.
- When there is no immediate risk, advice can be sought from the NSPCC in the UK (www.nspcc.org.uk), which provides information to professionals via a helpline as well as learning resources on topics such as Gillick competency to support decisions about the maturity of CYP.
- Speaking to the local authority in the client's area about your concerns without identifying the client is another way of obtaining advice and local information relevant to where they are located.

Therapeutic relationship and communicating with CYP in phone therapy

'Tenuous contact'

With some phone CYP clients, I think it is helpful to consider Pearce and Sewell's (2014) theory of adolescent process, which they describe as 'tenuous contact'. From having worked face to face in school settings, Pearce and Sewell noticed that for a young person, 'contact from session to session can feel new, difficult and tenuous'. Unlike the beginning of an adult session, there is no 'relational capital' and as young people tend to be focused on their experience in that moment, 'contact has to be established anew at each session; contact gained in previous sessions cannot be taken for granted' (2014, p. 28).

This approach resonates with me as phone therapy can feel tenuous with CYP. This might be because they don't speak or offer much or they might be chattier than adults, talking about what might seem like random subjects like shows, music, social media, superheroes or a pet which can leave therapists wondering about the therapeutic value of sessions and at times, feeling de-skilled.

Without full contact with the client, Pearce and Sewell describe the frustration therapists can feel which leads to clients being experienced as '"didn't want" or "inappropriate for" counselling'. They suggest consistency and low-level invitational contact over time. They believe in putting young people at the heart of the work as 'Young people are used to adults making relationships "about them" rather than the relationship being offered for use "on their terms"'.

One of the advantages of phone therapy is that without visual co-presence and the mystique of the therapy room, there can be a greater sense of equality for clients. Perhaps, a young client sounding distracted or the sound of scribbling, fidgeting or movement could become part of the relationship being more 'about them' than regarded by us as not giving therapy or indeed us the respect we might think is necessary. I have found that being more accepting of my client's autonomy and curious about what they share, how they share it and what enables them to share leads to a greater connection. As Pearce and Sewell contend, 'What's important is the "contact" rather than the "content" in each encounter'. It requires waiting until the client is ready and allowing the session to be more on their terms.

That said, as some young people don't readily bring up what was discussed in the previous session, it also means taking responsibility for returning to what was painful or hard for the client to say or difficult between the therapist and the client. Pearce and Sewell observe this saying that the client may act as if they have forgotten and the therapist 'may need to take sensitive and informed risks so that the possibility of a deepening relationship increases'. The risk of not doing this can exacerbate inequalities of power between the young person and adults.

Disclosure of difficult material

Without seeing the therapist or being seen, clients can feel uninhibited and safer to share what they find difficult to express. In my own practice with young people, this is most often connected to sexual abuse and sexual identity.

> *A long-term client who had experienced sexual abuse was able to use phone therapy at her own pace. Sessions usually started with what I experienced as tenuous contact as she moved about her room, talking about what she had in front of her, what she had just eaten or planned to eat, where she was going later and so on. She would also discuss the behaviour of her pets that were in the room with her and just talking about caring for them, their furriness and stroking them appeared to regulate her. I would wait for what would sometimes but not always come – a change in her pace and tone as she deftly dropped a memory, dream fragment, description of a trigger or experience of hypervigilance into the session which I would do my best to catch and hold gently as we explored it together. The client reported that talking on the phone about sexual abuse was easier for her than when we worked face to face. Sessions with this client were also shorter, and on the phone, the increased sense of equality made it easier for her to let me know when she wanted the session to end.*
>
> *Another client who I worked with face to face, on video and on the phone observed that they only discussed exploring their sexual identity when they had a phone session. They were able to describe the advantage of not feeling embarrassed to use particular words when they were not visible as well as not having to endure my gaze while they grappled with describing what felt shameful to them.*

Feeling able to express themselves more easily on the phone won't be experienced by all CYP clients. This could be due to anything such as psychological unsuitability, a disembodied voice being too stark for a young client or a client not liking the medium of the phone. Sometimes, freedom of expression isn't possible due to a lack of privacy and if you sense this, you might wonder about this with the CYP in a way that is safe for them, so that they need to only agree or disagree that this is the case. There might be room to discuss how more privacy could be obtained but when this isn't possible, use of video or a move to face-to-face therapy will be essential.

Communication and core skills

All of the communication and core skills described in Chapter 3 are relevant to working with CYP, some of the main points being:

- Consider your tone, pitch and intonation. I tend use a more expressive tone than I would with an adult, especially in the early sessions. Faking won't cut it with CYP, but considering the power imbalance, a friendly tone can help.

- Monitor the length of silences. A shorter silence on the phone is fairly typical anyway and when I work with young people, I 'notice' a silence sooner. The aim is not to end a silence but to maintain contact after which the silence might continue if it is reflective.
- Check the meaning to keep pace and verbal connection with the client. Checking meaning might be to ask the client to repeat a mumbled sentence or clarify understanding of youth culture and the slang that defines it. Location of self and willingness to be corrected as discussed in Chapter 7 on EDI can help level the playing field of intergenerational inequalities.
- Use encouragers. CYP might require more frequent audible nods or questions that facilitate and encourage sharing.
- Shorter sessions might be beneficial for CYP phone therapy clients for a number of reasons ranging from fast, disinhibited disclosure to age-related, shorter attention span or ADHD.
- End sessions well. This includes grounding the client as described in Chapter 8 or verbally expressed warmth and encouragement.

References

BACP. (2022). *BACP Competences for work with children and young people (4–18 years)*. www.bacp.co.uk/media/15873/bacp-cyp-competence-framework_2022.pdf

Equality Act 2010: Guidance. (2015, June 16). *Gov.UK*. www.gov.uk/guidance/equality-act-2010-guidance

Pearce, P., & Sewell, R. (2014, August 28). Tenuous contact: New theory about adolescent process. *Academia.Edu*. www.academia.edu/8111859/Tenuous_Contact_New_Theory_about_Adolescent_Process

Rattray, S. (2016). *Equality, diversity and inclusion (EDI) within the counselling professions, GPiA 063*. www.bacp.co.uk/media/10120/bacp-edi-within-counselling-professions-crp-gpia063-nov20.pdf

UKCP. (2021). *UKCP Guidelines for working online or remotely*. www.psychotherapy.org.uk/media/jrohoner/ukcp-guidelines-for-working-online-or-remotely-v1-0.pdf

For information and confidential advice on the application of the Equality Act on an individual level:

Equality Advice Service Tel: 0808 800 0082
www.equalityadvisoryservice.com

For advice on the interpretation of legislation and its application at an organisational level:

Equalities & Human Rights Commission Tel: 020 7832 7800 www.equality-humanrights.com/en

Chapter 8

Creative interventions for phone therapy

Working creatively with clients need not be restricted to face-to-face therapy. When I introduce the topic of creative interventions on my phone therapy training courses, there is usually a ripple of excitement. While some therapists are curious about how this is possible, others share their experience of using a variety of creative techniques.

What do we mean by creative interventions? Creative interventions are practised by qualified therapists holding a core training in their chosen theoretical orientation. Creative interventions in therapy are therefore different to the work of art therapists registered in the UK, who have an arts-based training as an art, drama, or music therapist and who use art, drama, or music as their primary mode of communication. Creative interventions are therefore not the preserve of art, drama or music therapists; indeed, Rosen and Atkins (2014) state that 'All counselors have basic training that enables them to approach their clients in creative ways' and furthermore, 'the arts belong to everyone in the service of life and healing'.

Using creative interventions with clients provides a way to dip into and explore the unconscious, from preverbal memories to current self-beliefs, without necessarily using words. Silverstone (1997) describes working creatively as accessing 'the world of spontaneous knowing, nothing to do with thoughts' during which the client creates 'an extension of the self in symbolic form made visible'.

Creative interventions can offer a wider channel through which clients are able to gain insight and express themselves. It becomes a way of working that is an extension of one of the phone's advantages – invisibility. Creative interventions facilitated by a therapist who remains unseen by the client can allow for greater exploration of difficult, shame-laden or embarrassing material by engaging with it in a different way that might not include words. On the phone, even a brief intervention such as an invitation to the client to explore the fantasy of 'If money was no object' or a visualisation such as 'If I had a second life' can be very effective. Perhaps, not being seen allows clients to share more deeply or share secret or unacknowledged desires more easily.

To explore creative phone therapy, I spoke to Tanja Sharpe, who, in 2016, founded Creative Counsellors, a network of therapists who compliment their

DOI: 10.4324/9781003253396-8

core modality of talking therapy with a range of creative interventions. Tanja, an integrative therapist and author of *Creative Counselling: Creative Tools and Interventions to Nurture Therapeutic Relationships* (Sharpe, 2022), explained that she noticed how clients can get stuck in trauma if they are expected to use words to process their experience. Using her own modality and incorporating creative skills, she notices significant change in clients, who she said 'move from stuck to express and engage'.

Some therapists might wonder how creative work is possible when you aren't in the same room and can't see the client. Please introduce this possibility to us.

Tanja: On phone, creative working can be very powerful because we don't see what our client is creating. When we look at somebody else's creation we have a barrier as we come from our own experience and history. When we work creatively, we aim to come from the client's own frame of reference. What we take from it is how the client describes what they are creating, we have no visual, only their voice telling us what they are seeing, what it feels like to them and what they want to do next. It's engaging, you tap into what the client is saying and you're imagining what they are creating, so I might say, 'Oh, I'm imaging from what you've described that is sounds like this' – you're mirroring and paraphrasing what you hear them saying. The client gets a lot from it because they take more time to relate to it to describe it than maybe they would if they were sitting with you, so there's a much deeper connection with the work. It is a different process to what happens in the room, and I absolutely love it.

How do you set your clients up for working creatively, how do you guide them and help them choose creative media?

Tanja: Creative working is an extension of talking therapy, an adaptation of the intervention with the client and I let them know this when I explain how I work in my online biography. There's a transparency right at the beginning which is part of the contracting with clients.

I will ask the client if and what kind of creativity and creative media interests them. They might already like to work with paints, story or poetry for instance and I explore this as part of the assessment. I specifically ask for anything they don't like to work with. We build a picture, a framework for how to choose different media for different exercises. I know what to avoid and what to suggest at different points of the work. Once we have done that, I give them a bit of a kit list. I might say 'When we work together have paper, pens, paints, water, paint brushes or clay' – whatever it is they want to work with, so they can dip in and out of various media. From that point it's really easy, I might suggest, 'I'm hearing you say it feels really awful for you to talk about, or tricky so I am just wondering if you'd like to be a bit curious and playful and create something around this?' If the client agrees, I'll ask 'I'm wondering what media you're drawn to with what you have there?' They might say, paper paints, pens and I'll say 'Just take a moment to get yourself set up, make a space for yourself, I'll give you a minute, let me know when you're ready'. So it's totally in their reference. They take their time, I don't see it, but I hear what they are doing because they tell me, they tend to describe a lot when you're on the phone – a lot more than when you're seeing them.

Does this mean that you don't see the work or does the client send you a photo?

Tanja: They quite often send a photo. Sometimes, they send it in between sessions and ask that we look at it together during the next session. At times, the bigger part happens when you're not in session with them. It's an extension of the exercise. It also happens a lot with journaling when the client creates artwork alongside their writing. I don't ask to see it; the client will tell me they really wish they could show me, and they send a photo by messaging or email and I open it and say, 'So what I am seeing is' with no interpretation. They are looking at it too and I might ask, 'Which part of your creation are you drawn to most?' We explore it together.

An art therapist might keep what the client had created. If the client is working remotely, they will be left with their creation and if it's an expression of anger or say related to trauma, couldn't this be difficult for them? How do you deal with this, particularly with young people who are at home?

Tanja: This is addressed during the contracting with clients and being clear at the beginning is the same as face-to-face therapy. Clients will create based on what will happen to it afterwards, it is an extension of the client, so how you treat that is important because it is like holding a part of them. On phone, in the contract I agree with clients that digital copies get printed and put in the file and then deleted digitally. Sometimes, I'll ask, 'What do you want me to do with this?' They might tell me to rip it up or burn it when the session is over. Because they know what will happen to it outside of the session, they can let the energy and their feelings go. This is important for clients who are young people but also for adults who are in difficult home life situations.

That's really helpful for therapists who want to incorporate artwork with phone therapy. What about other creative methods that can be transferred to the phone?

Tanja: Grounding and stabilisation work, tapping into all of the client's five senses, is great to do on the phone. It's helpful for clients who might be experiencing trauma. I might say to the client, 'Look around you for moment, what are you most drawn to in the room, what colour is it, what shape is it, if you were to touch it, what might it feel like. If you were to smell it, what might it smell like, would it be weird, what about if you were to taste it, would it be sweet?' You can bring a lot of laughter into the room to help someone re-stabilise. It's a really easy process on the phone.

Working with metaphor also works really well on the phone. For instance, 'If your anxiety was a shape or an object, is there something in the room that would represent it?' The client might say, 'My anxiety is like a lamp'. I would ask, 'What shape is it, how brightly does the anxiety turn up, how low can you dim the anxiety, what helps you to do that?' Working verbally with objects in the room is a creative process. We used to think that people used either their left brain or right brain, now functional magnetic resonance imaging (fMRI) shows that the whole brain lights up with blood flow when we are being creative. When you work creatively, you're engaging with all of the client's body and brain, you don't need to do artwork. You can do this by telling a story. If you are working with a young person you could ask, 'If you were a gaming character which character would you be, what superpower would you have? Are there any other characters in your game, do they relate to anyone else in life? Who is that like and how big is that character compared to your character?' All of this can be done verbally. It depends on how creative a therapist feels, how confident they feel to try it and the place to start is by being curious and playful because you never know where it's going to go.

It's about giving the client the invitation, they will either want to play or not.

Tanja: Yes, and it's also about working intuitively with what the client is really interested in. We don't have to share this interest, for example if they have a deck of angel cards, invite the client to open the cards, tell them to put aside the interpretation book as we're interested in the client's unconscious mind. Ask them to flip through the images and words and pick out the ones that stand out for them. We can then ask, 'Can you read them to me, describe the image, what colours stand out to you, what does that colour mean to you in your life, what emotion comes with that colour?' and so on.

What about working with music? During my phone therapy training, some therapists say they use music as part of therapy and this can be an active process, where their clients create music or a more passive one that involves listening or responding to music.

Tanja: I'm not musical but lots of therapist's do really wonderful sound therapy work. I just bring in the reference of music, if someone says I really like music it helps me chill out, I will say, 'Introduce me to your music'. We might play YouTube videos so I can hear the song, we'll talk about it and explore whether for them, maybe the lyrics are important. I might just reference it and ask if there is a specific band or a song that associates with that time in their life, so we have a verbal cue on it. You don't have to be an expert. It's about sticking to the client's frame of reference and music is very powerful.

I'm fascinated with doodling as creative expression during a session – my own and my clients. If my client says they have been doodling we discuss this, and it forms part of the work. Have you any thoughts on doodling?

Tanja: Doodling is the first creative work I do with clients. Everyone can do it; it smashes the block of 'I'm not creative'. People tend to think art is about something good enough to get put on a wall. Creativity in therapy is about the process, not the outcome. You might have a big ugly ball of clay, that has no shape to it, but you've pounded it, put all your feelings into it and that's all its going to be because that's all its meant to be as part of the process. Doodling is a fantastic for this. If people say they can't draw, they're not creative I ask them to close their eyes and draw, keep moving the pen on the paper, relax the breathing, slow it down, then look at what they've created. They can then add colour, words, cut things out of magazines and add to it and by the end, they have a landscape of whatever has been happening for them on the inside.

I find that Gloria Willcox's Feeling Wheel (Willcox, 1982) is helpful for clients who struggle to identify and describe their feelings. Is this something you would use, perhaps emailing it to the client for use during sessions?

Tanja: I love using Feeling Wheels with clients, but I suggest that clients don't buy into the colours. For example the colour red might not relate to them as being mad or angry. I send them a greyscale version so they can add colours that feel right for them.

Do you have any experience of working creatively with clients who identify as being neurodiverse? What would therapists need to bear in mind?

Tanya: I am neurodiverse myself as an ADHD counsellor and mum to my autistic son, so exploring ways to support neurodiverse clients is very important to me. With creative work, particularly when you can't see the client, you do need to be aware that sensory issues can be triggering. If during assessment and contracting a client says they're neurodiverse, I will ask about it to find out, for example, whether it is better for them to use gloves when they touch clay. Someone might be hypersensitive, where their senses seem too acute, and they need less stimulation as they are super sensitive, or they might be hyposensory, which means they need more stimulation, or they might be somewhere in the middle. One client I worked with who had olfactory hypersensitivity didn't like the smell of paint but liked essential oils. We discussed having a cotton wool pad with oils next to them. I use the assessment to find out about any blocks. Neurodiverse clients say they often don't get asked those things in talking therapy; perhaps, therapists are too timid to ask direct questions and clients like and want those direct questions.

I agree, phone therapy can give therapists greater freedom to ask direct questions because they can lean on the fact that they can't see the client and don't want to make assumptions.

Tanja: Therapists can ask direct questions and clients are free to share what they want. It's making me think, as the client doesn't have to show what they've created while they're on the phone, wondering whether the therapist thinks it's good, perhaps whether they're judging it – they are free to create and process uninhibitedly.

Tanja's experience demonstrates the potential for adapting a broad range of creative techniques for use on the phone. Like Tanja, I have found that clients are able to verbally describe what they draw or visualise, sometimes with a high level of detail, perhaps because of a combination of wanting you to understand fully and because they feel less inhibited knowing that you aren't able to see them or their creation. Being in their own space for their session need not mean that creative material or items are not so accessible to clients. Clients might use materials or items that hold significant meaning to them. This can make creative working a rich and powerful intervention for some clients.

My view is that just as therapists need to consider and adapt their modality and style of therapy for the phone, the same is true for working creatively without being physically present with a client. That said, it is essential for us to work with creative techniques in ways that are safe for clients. We always work within our level of competence and to ensure this, you might decide to undertake some creative therapy-based training.

Suggestions for safe creative working on the phone

- Think through how you will incorporate face-to-face creative interventions or new ideas for creative working into your phone therapy practice, what needs to be adapted when you work with voice alone. Consider how creative interventions will be discussed with and form part of your assessment, contracting, and boundary setting process.
- Offer phone-based techniques with full consideration of the client's circumstances on the day. Do they have enough privacy generally? Would another day be safer or feel more relaxed? This will be particularly important if the client decides to put the call on to speakerphone for greater freedom of movement. Ask whether this is the case.
- Extend the invitation to clients before starting to use a creative intervention. If you have a suggestion, ask whether they are willing to try it. Their answer will give you information about how they feel about the activity as well as how comfortable they are in their physical space.
- Get the timing right – if there isn't time to set up the activity, undertake it and have adequate time to discuss afterwards, leave it for another day. With some creative interventions, particularly those that require the client setting the activity up, allow more time than you would if you were in a face-to-face setting.
- The client needs to feel comfortable and know that what you're offering isn't something they need to get right or be good at. The technique is offered in the spirit of curiosity, experimentation or playfulness.

- Unless you are guiding a visualisation, creative interventions are offered in a non-directive, non-interpretive way. The focus is on what meaning the creation or expression holds for the client.
- All creative techniques are collaborative ventures. Visualisations and grounding exercises involve checking with the client during the process where necessary and gaining feedback afterwards.
- On the phone, always work with consideration of what will happen after the session. Discuss what the client will do next with a physical creation like a painting. Help the client consider good self-care and next steps – this might be about managing being alone or other people in the home after the session.

Using guided visualisations, metaphor, storytelling and other verbal creative techniques can be an accessible way for phone therapists to work if their clients don't have art-based materials available to them during the session. In my own practice, clients either email or simply talk about photographs, drawings and doodles, which help them access and process feelings, without me seeing them. Also, I work with clients who journal in between sessions or use other forms of creative writing including the technique of writing a letter that is not sent, which the client sometimes chooses to read during the session for us to explore together.

Michelle Nicholson's pluralistic phone therapy practice, see Chapter 4, demonstrates the powerful combination of expressive writing therapy combined with the client's uninhibited expression as they are unseen during phone sessions.

Expressive writing therapy

Michelle Nicholson is a pluralistic therapist who established a specialist phone therapy service in 2016 for women affected by hyperemesis gravidarum (HG), an extreme pregnancy sickness condition. Michelle now supervises other therapists who work for the UK charity Pregnancy Sickness Support as well as being employed as a therapist within a university. Drawing on research evidence showing that expressive and reflective writing can help people heal, recover from and make sense of difficult or traumatic life events, as well as on her own MSc research study, Michelle invited clients to engage with writing therapy where appropriate. She has published several papers on her findings including Writing therapeutically about chronic pregnancy sickness: women's perceptions of sufficiency (2017).

Michelle says,

> Writing therapy works well on the phone. Clients write between appointments and discuss the material as part of their session. They are invited to write as freely, deeply, and openly as possible about their pregnancy sickness experiences, thoughts and feelings without worrying about spelling, presentation, or grammar. They write either without prompts, whatever they feel they need or want to express, or choose from a list of suggestions sent in advance.

Examples of writing prompts include the following: write about your most vivid memories of pregnancy sickness; write about the kind of pregnancy you felt you wanted but didn't have; write a letter to your pregnancy sickness; write about who did and didn't understand your pregnancy sickness; write as if it were an object or image; or write how it is to be a pregnancy sickness survivor.

Michelle says that the benefits of writing therapy include an opportunity to write the unspoken before exploring further during a session where helpful, voicing the anger, validating the HG experience as real, externalising and venting the lived experience of HG and reclaiming agency.

Together with phone therapy, writing therapy has been a useful way for Michelle's clients to process the experience of HG. Phone therapy clients presenting with different issues might be attracted to expressive writing. This creative intervention, offered to and contracted with clients, could work well alongside phone therapy.

Visualisation

Many phone therapists find guided visualisation or guided imagery to be particularly effective on the phone. Therapists encourage clients to find a relaxed position, close their eyes and use verbal prompts to direct the focus of the imagery – mirroring the phone therapy setting. Perhaps, not being seen by the therapist allows the client to relax more easily and in their own homes, some clients might feel more comfortable sitting or lying down.

Whether visualisation is used to support clients to better manage anxiety, stress, pain, habits or strong feelings, therapists guide clients to close their eyes and notice the sensory aspects of the imagined scene – what a client might see, hear, smell, feel and taste.

As in any setting, the client is invited to participate in the visualisation. Without being able to monitor the client's body language, the therapist needs to set the scene, encouraging the client to let the visualisation unfold in a way that works for them, assuring them that they are in control and letting them know that they can give feedback or stop the visualisation at any time. Allow plenty of time for intervention in case there needs to be discussion to discuss the experience of client being in their own setting.

Without being able to see the client, it's wise to start with short visualisations of about five minutes to see how the experience was for the client, working together to discuss adjustments to make the process more comfortable.

Just as within a face-to-face setting, the process will involve helping the client to set themselves up for the intervention in a comfortable way, closing their eyes, feeling their body in contact with where they are sitting or lying, focusing on the breath before introducing the visualisation. End the visualisation by guiding the client back, helping them notice their body in contact with the chair or floor, hearing any noises around them, perhaps counting down to open their eyes and allowing time for them to bring their focus back to the present.

Integrative therapist, Andrea Howmans, who has also trained in Eye Movement Desensitisation and Reprocessing (EMDR), uses EMDR stabilisation techniques, such as self-regulation skills – grounding and self-soothing strategies which are suitable for phone therapy practice.

She incorporates them into a session to support a client in the present as well as guiding the client to practice the techniques independently outside of the session, without her direction. Andrea talks the client through finding a comfortable seated or reclining position before starting the techniques. Here are two examples.

The Light Stream Technique is a body scan used to identify and resolve distressing physical sensations and is particularly useful to help clients regulate their breathing towards the end of a session.

Andrea: I ask the client to concentrate on their upsetting bodily sensations. I then say, 'If the feeling had a shape, what would it be?' I then ask them to describe it further, 'If the feeling had a size and texture what would it be?' and 'Which of your favourite colours would it be? Choose a colour that is calm, peaceful and represents healing for you'. I guide them to feel their colour gently and easily entering through the top of their head, filling the shape of their body, talking them through this from head to toe. I ask the client for feedback during the process and if they say the visualisation is making a positive difference I continue, asking them to notice the warmth and peace throughout their body. To end, I guide the client back to the session on the count of five.

The second intervention, The Spiral Technique, can be helpful when clients are experiencing any physical disturbance in their body, often when they have been triggered by distressing or traumatic memories from the past.

Andrea: I ask the client to notice where the sensations of the memories are in their body. After this, I ask them to rate the experience from 1 to 10 with 10 being the highest level of disturbance. I then say, 'Imagine that the feelings or sensations are starting to turn' followed by 'Which direction are they moving, clockwise or counter clockwise?' I then ask them to, in their mind, turn the spiral in the other direction and notice what happens. If this technique works for the client, it allows for the disturbing feelings and memories to decrease. Like all interventions, if the client says there is no change, I'll choose another technique.

Grounding the client during phone therapy

Grounding a client, particularly after a difficult session, is useful whatever the setting. Grounded techniques can be really effective over the phone. For some clients, a quick, quirky, fun grounding technique is all that is needed. For others, enough time for a good ending in which both you and the client work together to regulate before the client enters their world at the end of a session is very important. There will be times when understanding the context and circumstances of a client's life immediately after each individual session will be very important. Helping them to centre, to consider how they will manage questions from a partner or parent or handle a meeting at work or the demands of putting children to bed, can go a long way to preparing them to avoiding feeling overwhelmed or vulnerable when you end the call.

In essence, the aim of grounding a client is to bring them back in touch with their body, with their senses, to the present moment in their immediate environment which is not the therapy room.

There are many ways to ground a client.

- Literal grounding – asking the client to dig their feet into the floor, noticing the contact, the tension, the aim being to remind the client that they are in touch with the ground beneath their feet.
- Seated body awareness – asking the client to notice the weight of their body in the chair, to wiggle their fingers and toes, the feel of the chair against their back, feet on the ground.
- Standing and mobile body awareness – getting up from the chair, bed or floor, stretching or clenching and releasing fists. Walking around the room to shift energy, big strides, little steps or walking on tip toe – whatever feels appropriate for that client in that moment.
- Breathing – for some, keep it simple by guiding the client to focus on their breathing, noticing each inhale and exhale, continue for ten slow, deep breaths. Alternatively, choosing from the many-staged, counting breathing exercises.
- My preference is 5–2–7 breathing which can be helpful with stress and anxiety:

  - 5 – count to five and breathe in through the nose.
  - 2 – hold the breath at its peak for two seconds.
  - 7 – slowly release the air in the lungs for seven seconds by making a small 'o' with your mouth.

- Noticing what is in the room – the client describes a favourite object or names a specific number of items such as those of a similar colour or shape. Ask them to read out the title and author of three books on the bookshelf or describe the cat on the sofa next to them or a picture on the wall or the style of the furniture in the room.
- Noticing the outdoor environment – ask the client to look out of the window and describe the scene. This is better still if they are outdoors when they can tell you what they see, hear and smell.
- Draw upon the client's interests – name five Marvel characters, six perennial plants, seven favourite types of food or as many footballers you can name in one minute, for instance.
- What the client will do after the session – this brings them right into their immediate environment. It might be sitting awhile, making a cup of tea, stepping out into the garden, listening to music or taking the dog for a walk.

Working collaboratively with clients, assessing, contracting, agreeing to boundaries, holding the frame are all essential elements of working creatively. So too is holding a non-directive, non-interpretive stance in mind. Creative interventions work well on the phone – plan your creative intervention toolkit, discuss it with your supervisor if you are unsure and always offer an intervention as a choice to clients.

References

Nicholson, M. (2017). Women's experiences of the therapeutic value of writing about pregnancy sickness. *Counselling and Psychotherapy Research*, *18*(1), 26–34. https://doi.org/10.1002/capr.12151

Rosen, C. M., & Atkins, S. S. (2014). Am I doing expressive arts therapy or creativity in counseling? *Journal of Creativity in Mental Health*, *9*(2), 292–303. https://doi.org/10.1080/15401383.2014.906874

Sharpe, T. (2022). *Creative counselling: Creative tools and interventions to nurture thera-peutic relationships*. Jessica Kingsley Publishers.

Silverstone, L. (1997). *Art therapy – the person-centred way: Art and the development of the person* (2nd ed.). Jessica Kingsley.

Willcox, G. (1982). The feeling wheel: A tool for expanding awareness of emotions and increasing spontaneity and intimacy. *Transactional Analysis Journal*, 274–276.

Chapter 9

Considerations for supervision by phone

As this is a book on phone therapy, this chapter offers only a brief overview of phone therapy supervision. As a supervisor, I work with supervisees on the phone that I have never met face to face and just as with phone therapy, in my experience, developing a supervisory alliance using voice alone is completely possible. My view is that supervision by phone is modelled on face-to-face supervision but with some key differences that will be explored here.

Phone supervision has a number of advantages over a face-to-face setting. Without the need to be located within commuting distance, phone supervision provides access to a larger number of supervisors allowing for a better specialism, expertise or relational fit. There can be greater flexibility and continuity of sessions by permitting party freedom to move location either temporarily or permanently. There are also other advantages such as lack of travel time and cost to meet face to face, no room hire costs and as a result, to potentially schedule earlier or later session times.

Phone supervision or supervision on the phone?

Weitz (2018) highlights the difference between online supervision and supervision online. Whether face-to-face therapists receive online supervision or online therapists receive online supervision, digital working is involved and the implications of this need to be carefully considered and prepared for. Indeed, Weitz points out that 'the majority of psychological therapists and their supervisors are working face to face but having some digital impact on their work even if not working online' (Weitz, 2018, p. 145). This might be anything from emailing clients or storing data online which has been discussed in Chapters 2 and 5. Whether phone supervisors provide supervision for phone therapy or face-to-face therapy, digital implications need to be considered. A key difference, however, is the need to be mindful of all that comes into play when a client is not physically present with a supervisee.

Models of online supervision

Starting from the wider perspective of online supervision, Stokes (2018, p. 29) asserts that most models can be used for online therapy as long supervisors think

DOI: 10.4324/9781003253396-9

through any aspects that would not transfer and make plans to adapt or add to models accordingly.

The four models of supervision listed here have been adapted for online supervision – video, email (synchronous and asynchronous), text (live chat) and some reference to audio.

- Weitz's (2019) adaptation of Inskipp and Proctor's (1993) supervision alliance model to include six dimensions in online supervision – the supervisory alliance, the normative/managerial, the formative/educative, supportive/restorative, digital health technologies and the relational dimension
- O'Brien's (2018, p. 39) adaptation of Hawkin's (Hawkins & Shohet, 1989) CLEAR model – Contract, Listen, Explore, Action and Review
- Mosson's (2018, p. 45) adaptation of Clarkson's FORUM model – Foundation, Online Transference, Restorative, Uninhibited, Meaning
- Collin's (2018, p. 54) CARER model, which she describes as an 'overlap' of a number of models for example Inskipp and Proctor's Supervision Alliance Model (1993), Bernard and Goodyear's (2004) discrimination model, Page and Wosket's (2001) cyclical model and Hawkins and Shohet's (1989) CLEAR model

These adapted models offer some helpful perspectives and approaches and incorporate use of technology, confidentiality and data security, language and communication and working with online psychological processes, assessing suitability for working remotely, managing risk, referral pathways and working internationally.

Adapting face-to-face supervision for the phone

It is not the purpose of this chapter to propose a new or adapt any one existing model of supervision for working without seeing a supervisee. Generic models of supervision provide the potential for a wide range of choice for phone therapy across all theoretical orientations and I have included some of these perspectives here. My suggestion is that supervisors reflect on their face-to-face supervision practice, consider which model or models they use the most and find most helpful in their work before thinking about what needs to be adapted to best fit the medium of the phone.

In my own practice, the task of supervision varies depending on the experience of my supervisees as therapists as well as their experience of being a phone therapist. This means that the range of the work includes discussion about anything from phone therapy contracts to exploring assumptions without seeing the client.

As with phone clients, without sight I aim to extend a warm verbal welcome to new supervisees, being aware of the need to start building the relationship between us as quickly as possible. The supervisee will have received my contract for supervision in advance and even though questions will have been invited by email before the first session, I ask the supervisee whether they would like me to clarify any matters or discuss our agreement. Negotiating happens verbally and in writing.

After this, depending on how much I already know about the supervisee, I enquire about their work, their theoretical orientation, the context – private practice or organisation, whether the therapy they provide is short term or ongoing, which settings are used – the phone, online or face to face and whether the work is blended. Gauging their level of experience as a face-to-face practitioner as well as their knowledge of and familiarity with working on the phone helps me begin to shape what they might need from supervision. Reflecting on the apprenticeship model of Hawkins and Shohet (1989), it is possible for a supervisee to be at master craftsperson level with a high level of experience or a knowledgeable journeyperson in their face-to-face practice but feeling less confident or competent when working without being physically present, certain elements of their practice will be explored at apprentice or even novice level during supervision.

Through the lens of Inskipp and Proctor's (1993) supervision alliance model, I begin to think about the supervisee's current requirement for *formative, normative restorative* supervision. Every practitioner needs all three of course, but a supervisee who is new to phone therapy might need more of a *formative* element to start with, during which we might consider skills and professional development for working on the phone without visual cues. A supervisee might approach me for phone supervision after starting work for an agency offering phone therapy, an EAP for instance. In this case, more *normative* supervision might be an initial focus during which we might consider compliance with organisation procedures, adapting to a particular model, say short-term phone therapy for which we will discuss developing the best practice and any legal or ethical considerations for the context of work.

Sometimes, a new supervisee's greatest initial need is *restorative*. Not being seen by a supervisor and the part disinhibition plays without visual cues can allow for heartfelt sharing after a particularly challenging situation, perhaps one in which we discuss vicarious trauma. These matters need to be spoken of, listened to deeply and received unreservedly before anything else and this sharing will lay the foundation stones of the working alliance. That said, all therapists need *restorative* supervision. Without a doubt, in addition to being rewarding, invigorative and life enhancing, our work as therapists in any setting can be demanding, frustrating, baffling and anxiety provoking. Phone therapy can be intense and draining at times using only our sense of hearing, just as online therapy can lead to screen fatigue. The *restorative* element to supervision helps the supervisee consider the impact of the work and provides them with essential psychological and professional support to help relieve stress and attend to their own well-being and self-care.

Without physical presence, there is a need to verbally communicate warmth and demonstrate positive regard for the supervisee's work. Unless there is evidence otherwise, we convey the belief that the supervisee has good intentions and goodwill towards their work. Remote working requires a more collaborative approach and I think that phone supervision for phone therapy needs to be a collegial endeavour. Supervision is a balance of support and challenge but without visual cues, verbal reassurance and a non-judgemental attitude go a long way to encourage open and honest sharing. Listening deeply, using audible nods to indicate validation of what is being presented, sets the scene for a mutual sharing of ideas. Without sight, being curious about the supervisee's sense of the client by asking how they experienced an encounter, how they view it, what they feel about it and how they came to a particular conclusion is a powerful way to demonstrate this. Questions and exploration of this nature are what occurs during mode 3, the third eye of Hawkins and Shohet's (2013) seven-eyed model of supervision, the relationship between the client and the supervisee.

To acknowledge the experience of how it feels to work with clients using hearing and voice alone comes as a relief for supervisees. Just as with phone therapy clients, trust can develop quickly, and this advantage helps establish a safe and respectful relationship in which exploration and disclosure can take place. This is vital at certain times, perhaps management of client risk (Inskipp & Proctor's, 1993) (*normative* function) or review of the relationship between supervisor and supervisee (Hawkins & Shohet's, 2013) (mode 5, the fifth eye's focus on supervisory relationship).

Just as with phone clients, in the absence of body language, a lot of detailed material can be shared quickly by supervisees. The pace of supervision, especially if a supervisee has strong feelings towards the client, can lead to the fast presentation of a case. Perhaps, a supervisee has been on the receiving end of a client's disinhibited response or maybe the supervisee feels discomfort and concern about having a disinhibited reaction to a client. I try to interrupt flow as little as possible to start with, responding with verbal gestures to demonstrate understanding. I attempt patient tuning in and acknowledgement, demonstrating empathy, attempting to remember Hawkins and Shohet's (2013) assertion of, 'Never know better and never know first'. I might, however, butt in to clarify understanding to avoid assumptions. I am alert for signs of embarrassment, watching out for shame, noticing any defensiveness if I ask a question. I keep an ear out for changes in tone or pitch, hesitations or pauses.

Psychodynamic orientations will consider it is essential for supervisees to explore all forms of transference and countertransference. This can be done in ways similar to when working face to face, like as suggested Hawkins and Shohet's (2013, p. 96) mode 4, the fourth eye, the sharing of the supervisee's spontaneous responses to 'Who does this person remind you of' and what they would want to say to that person before describing ways that the client is different to that person. By contrast, Tudor and Worrall (2010, p. 72) state that a person-centred modality might explore this as the client's 'interpersonal strategies, secondary to their fragile process, rather than as an unconscious defence' during supervision. Their view is that person-centred therapy and practice will focus on acceptance and understanding, the same as any other attitude of the client (2010, p. 72). How disinhibition is regarded and explored in supervision will vary, the important point here is that its expression can be activated very powerfully on the phone.

The supervisor's internal responses have an important role in understanding what is going on for the supervisee and the client. Wosket (1999, p. 225) states that 'parallel process in supervision is frequently activated by the supervisor's internal responses – thoughts, feelings, sensations, fantasies, images – to what the supervisee is presenting'. On the phone, exploring parallel process can be an exciting revelation for both supervisee and supervisor and at times a real conundrum. Even though you can't see the supervisee or their client, the fantasies, feelings and sensations Wosket describes are experienced vividly and strongly, which, in an environment of trust can be explored energetically and provide valuable insight for the supervisee.

Use of self in supervision, just as in therapy, has its rewards and risks. Sometimes, we might exercise restraint and hold back until we process our own feelings. Like phone therapy, phone supervision can allow for a degree of physical relaxation and unseen facial expressions. Wanlass (2013, p. 222) shares the following, 'As when conducting psychoanalysis where I am in a state of reverie outside the analysand's visual field, sometimes I like the private space where I can react outside the supervisee's gaze, as it provides more space for thinking'.

Without visual cues it might be wise to check understanding to avoid assumptions before sharing with a supervisee. I am mindful of Hawkins and Shohet (2013, p. 80) asserting, 'We often find that we say things to our supervisees that we need to learn. It is as if our mouth is more closely linked to our subconscious knowing than was our metal apparatus'. As the pace of phone sessions can be faster than face to face, we might need time outside of the supervision session to process what occurred before sharing it. Sharing an unrestrained account of an experience and our feelings about it in our own supervision can help us see the wood for the trees. Wosket (1999, p. 217) writes of using her own supervision as well as having learnt that she needs to spend time with her feeling and 'get through it sufficiently to emerge the other side into clearer air that will give me some thinking space'.

Sometimes, it takes courage to throw into the ring a thought or comment from our own response and without sight to see how this lands. After mutual exploration of the response in relation to the supervisee and client, checking out how it was received, 'How was it for you to hear me say that?' This will be especially important if you notice a pause or silence, or you hear a change of tone of the supervisee's voice or a non-verbal sound. Sometimes, we might intuit this. Wanlass, 2013, p. 222 observes,

> Periodically, the lack of visual contact frees me up to imagine how the supervisee might respond, such as a moment where I envision an eye roll through the phone line. So, the telephone creates both a loss and a potential space.

Checking in and checking out with the supervisee can help mitigate the loss of visual cues and iron out any unwitting bluntness of your exchange or turn of phrase.

The BACP supervision competence framework (2021) includes the important component of 'fostering an egalitarian relationship with supervisees' reminding us that we need the 'Ability to discuss with the supervisee the inherent power difference within the supervisory relationship with the aim of: promoting the supervisee's autonomy, helping the supervisee to manage their own part in the supervisory power dynamic'. It doesn't end there however as we are also tasked with balancing this with an 'Ability to anticipate and manage the tensions between egalitarianism and supervisor responsibilities such as those relating to gatekeeping and the management of risk'.

I aim to provide a safe, non-judgemental space to supervisees, to encourage their sharing. Also, there will be a mutual sharing of ideas. I trust that they will bring the things they need to explore to sessions and the starting point is their sense, their experience. I might say, 'You were in the session with the client, tell me more about how you experienced it, how you view it, say a little more about how you came to that conclusion'. Qualified therapists make autonomous decisions for which I am not responsible. My role is to bolster supervisees, so they feel confident, make well-considered, justifiable ethical decisions or interventions.

Contracting and practicalities for supervision by phone

A written supervision working agreement setting out the terms, context and parameters of work and the relationship can be sent to prospective supervisees in advance and discussed between both parties as they start working together. Defining the supervisory relationship and clarity of the roles, expectations, practical considerations, rights and responsibilities of the supervisor and supervisee is the starting point for the alliance between both parties and ensures that the client is held safely at the heart of the work.

Typically, written and verbal contracting for phone supervision will include:

- Frequency and duration of sessions
- Who will phone whom
- Arrangements for backup plan in case of technical failure
- Limits to confidentiality and ethical considerations
- Cancellation policy
- What constitutes a DNA, will the supervisor be available for part or the whole of the session
- Availability for contact between sessions
- How sessions will be paid for and

- How writing of reports or other documentation relating to the supervision will be managed
- Arrangements for working with any other stakeholders, student placement co-ordinator for example

Having knowledge and understanding of the key elements of working legally, professionally and ethically on the phone is essential. At various points of the work with supervisees, from initial contracting with clients to managing legalities and at times of risk, there will be the need to incorporate the considerations covered in Chapter 5.

Discussion with supervisees about working legally, professionally and ethically will include:

- Main security issues for the provision of phone therapy – client privacy, the risk of eavesdropping, phone hacking, inadvertent recording of sessions and other confidentiality breaches
- When online security is relevant for phone therapy – data security, password protection, security updates, Wi-Fi and hotspots and receiving payment online
- Technology implications when managing higher levels of risk, the threat of domestic abuse for instance
- The supervisee's digital footprint – their online listing, website, web presence and use of social media
- Adequate insurance cover for the provision of phone therapy
- The legal implications of working internationally

Right from the start, providing and receiving supervision on the phone creates an opportunity for open discussion about working with clients using the medium. This might be the supervisee's phone therapy contract with clients, how well headset microphones are working, how much can be heard if the supervisee moves or any distractions such as an echo in the room or noise from elsewhere in the supervisees house. Frank feedback about practicalities during supervision can be invaluable as clients might not feel able to raise an issue.

Helping the supervisee develop communication skills for phone therapy

All of the skills included in Chapter 3 Communication and core phone therapy skills which are needed to form and maintain an effective therapeutic relationship can be drawn on and explored with the supervisee, including:

- Use of voice – reflection on the client's pitch, tone and intonation with the supervisee as well as observation of the supervisee's use of voice, including their non-verbal communication

- Managing any client colloquialisms and linguistic considerations including high rising terminal and creaking voice
- Conveying empathy in the absence of presence, with voice alone
- Establishing and developing the relationship, maintaining psychological contact verbally by using encouragers and audible nods
- Developing trust
- Making contact with less communicative clients and maintaining contact with fast talkers
- Recognising feelings without visual cues, facilitating crying and handling strong emotions
- Dealing effectively with silences
- Matching and monitoring client pace
- Considering and managing the presentation of introversion and extroversion
- Working with psychological processes – recognising and managing client and therapist disinhibition, assumptions, working with heightened feelings of fantasy and speculation

Equality, diversity and inclusion (EDI) as part of phone supervision

Equality is about fairness and apportioning equal value and worth to all supervisees and clients. In the UK, the starting point for assimilating EDI into our practice is the Equality Act (2010), which specifies nine protected characteristics which need to be borne in mind whatever the setting or context of supervision, see Chapter 7.

EDI needs to be at the heart of our therapy practice. It requires that supervisors understand and respect diversity and are aware of how differences and similarities can affect power dynamics in supervisory relationships. In addition to this, supervision needs to be a safe space in which supervisees can explore their emotional responses to equality, diversity and inclusion, including unconscious bias around difference (BACP supervision competence framework, 2021).

Supervision is also the place to explore intersectionality, considering how race, class, gender and other individual characteristics 'intersect' with one another and overlap. This requires self-awareness, willingness to engage in EDI-related professional development and an openness to sometimes discuss difficult subject matter without collapsing into shame as described by Anthea Benjamin in Chapter 7.

Key EDI discussions in supervision are likely to include:

- Not making assumptions when there are no visual cues
- Asking EDI-related questions during the assessment
- Developing the skill of asking questions in a sensitive manner as clients disclose information or the supervisee senses difference and diversity

- Considering levels of self-disclosure to the client, for instance, the supervisee's race, gender and class
- The effects of disinhibition, perhaps levels and tone of disclosure by the client and a supervisee's uninhibited reaction to a client regarding EDI issues

Psychological suitability and managing risk during supervision

Supporting supervisees to assess the appropriateness of phone therapy for a client is an important part of the work. Gauging psychological suitability, managing and acting on risk at a distance without visual cues is detailed in Chapter 6. An understanding of the following is required to support supervisees:

- Establishing the client's identity and obtaining contact information necessary for phone therapy, including personal, GP and person to contact in case of emergency. Adapting a face-to-face assessment for use on the phone including any additional questions which might be helpful when working without seeing the client, examples in Chapter 6
- Use of questionnaires and outcome measures and suggestions for balancing an appropriately thought through assessment against the need to rapidly build a relationship when not in the room
- Helping the supervisee prepare in advance by thinking through scenarios they haven't encountered on the phone before, for example breaches of privacy and interruptions, agreeing the setting with different clients, young people, for instance boundary setting
- Appraising and monitoring risk – the setting, technology and the client's mental and physical health
- Assessing psychological suitability on a case-by-case basis, supporting the supervisee to gain clarity about why the phone might not be an appropriate setting for a client whether it is because of psychological vulnerability, the limits of short-term contract, a risk due to a lack of privacy or perhaps level of experience or competence of the supervisee
- Assessing risk and safeguarding issues when the supervisee is not physically present with the client. Supporting them as they balance the therapeutic relationship, confidentiality and legal and ethical considerations, discussing how waivers of confidentiality are worded and managing risk as a continuous process
- Supporting the supervisee in times of risk, establishing responsibility in cases of risk, who they might approach for additional information such as services local to the client, how they will respond including whether to report safeguarding concerns for legal, contractual or ethical reasons. Thinking through options and actions in advance of immediate risk situations by asking 'What will you do if' or working through the Risk Management Plan prompts in Chapter 6

- Helping the supervisee think through when and how to refer clients to other or additional services or support. This might include considering how to research agencies local to the client and how to discuss this with the client in ways that are not rejecting and holding the client's safety and best interest at heart
- Providing restorative supervision especially after an incident of risk to help the supervisee process learning and think through any changes to their practice. Supporting the supervisee by providing a safe, non-judgement space to debrief and offering reassurance and encouragement

Understanding the context and legal implications of the supervisee's work

If the supervisee works for an organisation the contract will usually be between the organisation and the supervisor, but a self-employed supervisee providing therapy to clients via an agency could be responsible for their own supervision requirements. This means that the level of direct information about and involvement in phone therapy provision, policy and processes will vary. Supervisees working for an organisation will be working within defined protocols regarding contracting, assessment, flagging and monitoring risk, limits to the number of sessions and frequency of use of outcome measure questionnaires. Supervision will support the supervisee navigate their practice around organisational policy and their autonomy. By contrast, supervisees in private practice will be thinking through and making decisions on all elements of their phone therapy practice. Supervision will include supporting the supervisee with the challenges and advantages of both contexts.

Understanding the parameters of responsibility to the supervisee and the client is important, especially if the phone supervision is being provided for phone therapy. Phone therapy for some client groups will need careful consideration during supervision about legalities and ethics.

For instance working with children and young people on the phone requires knowledge of legal frameworks, awareness of professional and ethical guidelines, particularly around confidentiality, consent and capacity and supporting the supervisee to make informed judgements, see Chapter 7. The organisational context will influence decisions about safeguarding, managing risk and information sharing. Professional bodies will have their own guidelines on supervising work with children and young people. The BACP has recently updated their CYP (4–18 years) competence framework to include competences for online and phone therapy (OPT).

Another area is working internationally, see Chapter 5. Researching the law and mental health provision of a prospective client's country as well as thinking about how to manage two different legal systems are two obvious areas of discussion in supervision. If phone supervision is offered to supervisees located and working in other countries, multicultural dimensions come into play. Wanlass (2013, p. 216) writes of her experience as a 'distance supervisor'.

> I knew very little about Mongolia or Mongolian mental health treatment prior to my graduate student's sudden relocation to this region. With the assistance of my student, I quickly educated myself to help her provide culturally sensitive mental health practice. The supervisor must rely in part on the supervisee to educate the supervisor regarding social issues and common practices, which has an effect on the supervisory dynamic. The power differential is significantly lessened, as in some ways the supervisor becomes the student of the supervisee.

Choosing a phone therapy supervisor

Much is written elsewhere about how to find a supervisor which can feel complex considering the potential for them to hold a great deal of influence and, in some instances power over a supervisee. Above all else, the choice needs to be someone who is able to build and develop safe, respectful, supportive and honest relationships with supervisees. Someone who allows supervisees to bring whatever they feel they need to supervision and works collaboratively with them. Both supervisee and supervisor are humans of course and the relationship will require maintenance and monitoring at times. Although it can be challenging to both parties, unconscious influences and parallel processes occur and the ability to reflect on this on occasion is necessary. So too is sharing and accepting differences in views, beliefs, culture and backgrounds during the sessions.

Regarding the medium of the phone, here are my suggestions for selecting a phone supervisor:

- Choose a supervisor with experience of working on the phone specifically, or in addition to online via video, email and text.
- Choose someone who actually likes the medium of the phone, who values it. Someone who regards phone therapy as equal to other therapy settings as opposed to only being used in the case of technology failure.
- Choose a supervisor who, having experience of and belief in the medium, views phone supervision as a collaborative venture. Someone who is able to understand the nuances of the client's voice, pace and silences. Someone who can work collegially with you and share their sense of the work through use of self as well as on occasion use self-disclosure in the best interests of offering you formative, normative and restorative supervision.
- Choose a supervisor who is responsive and understands and has experience of facilitating supervisees to assess, monitor and manage risk.

- Someone who understands blended work – including the practical, contractual elements of providing a combination of phone, face-to-face and online therapy and who understands the psychological processes that can occur in these different settings.

References

BACP. (2021). *BACP supervision competence framework I*. www.bacp.co.uk/media/10930/bacp-supervision-competence-framework-feb21.pdf

Bernard, J. M., & Goodyear, R. K. (2004). *Fundamentals of clinical supervision* (3rd ed.). Boston: Allyn & Bacon.

Collins, L. (2018). New models of online supervision – (3) Carer. In *Online supervision: A handbook for practitioners* (1st ed., pp. 54–61). Routledge.

Hawkins, P., & Shohet, R. (1989). *Supervision in the helping professions*. Open University Press.

Hawkins, P., & Shohet, R. (2013). *Supervision in the helping professions* (4th ed.). Open University Press.

Inskipp, F., & Proctor, B. (1993). *The art, craft & tasks of counselling supervision*. Cascade Publications.

Mosson, S. (2018). New models of online supervision – (2) Breaking news! Face to face supervision and online supervision are not the same!! In *Online supervision: A handbook for practitioners* (1st ed., pp. 45–53). Routledge.

O'Brien, M. (2018). New models of online supervision – (1) Clear. In *Online supervision: A handbook for practitioners* (1st ed., pp. 39–44). Routledge.

Page, S., & Wosket, V. (2001). *Supervising the counsellor: A cyclical model* (2nd ed.). Routledge.

Stokes, A. (2018). Meandering through models: Can face to face models of supervision be used for online supervision? In *Online supervision: A handbook for practitioners* (1st ed., pp. 29–38). Routledge.

Tudor, K., & Worrall, M. (2010). *Freedom to practice: Person-centred approaches to supervision* (2nd ed.). PCCS.

Wanlass, J. (2013). Technology-assisted supervision and consultation. In J. Savege Scharff (Ed.), *Psychoanalysis online: Mental health, teletherapy, and training* (pp. 215–225). Karnac Books.

Weitz, P. (2018). Supervision guideline: Online supervision and supervision online – what's the difference? In *Online supervision: A handbook for practitioners* (1st ed., pp. 130–146). Routledge.

Weitz, P. (2019). *Online supervision using digital health technologies: The six-dimension model*. from https://dclinpsych.leeds.ac.uk/wp-content/uploads/sites/26/2021/03/Online-Supervision-using-Digital-Health-Technologies.pdf

Wosket, V. (1999). *The therapeutic use of self: Counselling practice, research and supervision* (1st ed.). Routledge.

Index

Note: Locators in *italic* indicate boxes.

accessibility, phone therapy and therapy supervision 13–14, 45, 48, 57, 65, 91, 101, 106, 126
Aeschlimann, Melanie 8, 30
age, older people 106–107
alcohol dependency 49, 85–86
anger 5, 31–32, 93, 102, 105; *see also* disinhibition/disinhibition effect
anonymity: dissociative 33; visual 15–16, 33
Antonioni, David Thomas 1, 25
anxiety 13; client 47, 72, 118; therapist 13, 18, 27, 30, 78
assessment 73–82, 83; adaptation to phone therapy 73–74; client identity, contact details 73; psychological suitability 78–79; risk assessment, immediate risk management plan 76–82, 82, 111; therapy-related questions 74–76
assumptions, avoiding 18, 23, 37–38, 93, 99, 103–104, 133
auditory system, ear 2, 3, 5, 6, 95, 97; pathway of sound 3–4; peripheral system 3

BACP: Ethical Framework for the Counselling Professions (2018) 57, 58, 81; Good Practice in Action (2020) 59; Online and Phone Therapy (OPT), competence framework (2021) 12–13, 24, 33, 35, 55, 56, 65, 72, 78
Balick, Aaron 55
BAME communities; *see* race and culture
Bedi, Robinder P. 25–26
Bell, Alexander Graham 4, 10
Benjamin, Anthea 98–102

bias, unconscious bias 37–38, 90, 97–98, 133
blended therapy 87–88
body language 18, 23, 25–26, 28, 45–46, 94, 95, 122
British Association for Counselling and Psychotherapy; *see* BACP
Broadbent, Donald E. 6

Children Act (1989)/Adoption and Children Act (2004) 81, 111
children and young people (CYP) 46–47, 108–114; boundaries, therapeutic space 109–111; client assessment 110–111; communication and core skills 113–114; contracting 108–109; difficult material, disclosure 113; guidelines and training 108; legal framework, ethical guidelines 81, 135; phone habits 15; privacy 49, 67; safeguarding, risk assessment/ management 81, 111; tenuous contact 112, 113; therapeutic relationship and communicating 112–114
Cocktail Party Effect 6–7
cognitive behavioural therapy (CBT) 50–51
confidentiality: client–therapist, extend and limits 61, 64–65, 73, 81, 101–102, 109, 111, 134; vs disclosure duties 61, 81; and security, technological 53–56, 97, 109, 111
contract 57–59, 57–70; arrangements for sessions 59–60; cancellations, non-attendance 62; confidentiality 61–62; fees, fee payment 61–62; informed consent 57; verbal contracting 57, 59, 66–67; written 57, 59, 60, 67, 76
countertransference, transference 44–45, 46, 88, 129

COVID-19 1, 11–12, 14, 40, 43, 45, 47, 85, 108
creaking voice 22–23, 132
creative interventions 115–125; contracting and process 116; creative techniques and media 116–118; creative techniques/media 120; define, concept 115; expressive writing therapy 121–122; grounding techniques 121, 123–124; neurodiversity and 119; safe creative working, suggestions 120; visualisation 47, 85, 115, 121, 122–123
crying 29–30

Day, Susan X. 16, 26–27
dichotic listening task, experiment 6
disability 91–95; assessment fatigue 92; 'disability spread' 92–93; permission statement 92–93, 94; phone therapy, suitability 91–92; social vs medical model 92, 93
disinhibition, disinhibition effect: client 14, 33–35, 41, 75, 79–80, 84, 102, 105, 113, 129; therapist 36–37
Drew, Paul 50–51
drug addiction 49, 85–86
Duff, Carlton T. 25
Dunn, Dana S. 87

ear; see auditory system, ear
eating disorders 82–85
Eye Movement Desensitisation Reprocessing (EMDR) 123
Emberson, Lauren 7
emergency, emergency contacts 17–18, 61, 73, 80, 82; see also risk management
Emilion, Jessie 98–102
empathy, communicating 21, 25, 41, 133
equality, diversity and inclusion (EDI) 23, 90–114; age, older people 106–107; children and young people (CYP) 108–114 (see also children and young people (CYP)); disability 91–95; gender, sexual and relationship diversity (GSRD) 103–106; hearing loss 95–98; race and culture, non-native speakers 23, 98–102
Equality Act (2010) 90
ethics, ethical phone therapy 53; BACP Ethical Framework for the Counselling Professions (2018) 57, 58, 81; children and young people, safeguarding 81, 108, 135; client assessment of psychological

suitability 78–79, 134; GDPR, consent and adherence 56; professional code 62; see also legal consideration and obligations
extroverts 28, 133

face-to-face counselling vs phone therapy 1, 16, 17–19, 25, 41–43, 43–45, 45–47, 48–49
Farmer, Joanna 40–43
fast talker 26–27, 28, 133
Feeling Wheel 119

Gaskell, Linda 45–47
gender, sexual and relationship diversity (GSRD) 103–106; acceptance/safety signalling 103, 104; heteronormative thinking 100; identity disclosure 103, 104; societal rejection, embarrassment 105–106; therapist's self-education, assumptions 103–104; voice dysphoria 105
General Data Protection Regulation (GDPR, 2018) 56, 61, 64–65
grounding techniques 117, 121, 123–124
Grumet, Gerald W. 15
GSRD identity; see gender, sexual and relationship diversity (GSRD)

Halacre, Mel 91–95
'halfalogues' 7
hearing: define, process 2–3; hearing loss 95–98; human sound as emotional trigger 2, 8; reliability in therapy 1; sound as emotion trigger 4; see also auditory system, ear
Hebbrian plasticity 7, 7–8
helplines vs phone therapy, differences 11–12
Hill, Julie 82–86
Holdgraf, Christopher R. 7–8
Horowitz, Seth 2, 21
Howmans, Andrea 123
hyperemesis gravidarum (HG), counselling 48–49

immediate risk management plan 82, 111
integrative transpersonal 45–47
integrative transpersonal psychotherapy 45–47
intimacy of phone as medium 2, 6, 15, 18, 34, 41–42, 44, 47

intonation; *see* vocal characteristics (pitch, tone intonation)
introverts 28, 133
Irvine, Annie 1, 50–51

Jung, Carl Gustav 28

Leach, Siwan 106–107
legal consideration and obligations 63–65, 132, 135–136; Care Act (2014) 81; Children Act (1989)/Adoption and Children Act (2004) 81, 111; confidentiality vs disclosure duties 61, 81; data protection 64–65; duty-of-care requirements, workplace 81, 61; Equality Act (2010) 90, 133; General Data Protection Regulation (GDPR) and the Data Protection Act (2018) 56, 61, 64–65; insurance 64; international work 63–64; Mental Capacity Act (2005) 81; safeguarding 79, 81, 111; *see also* contract
LGBTQ+/LGBTQIA+; *see* gender, sexual and relationship diversity (GSRD)

misophonia 5
modality adaptation for phone therapy 40–51; cognitive behavioural therapy (CBT) 50–51; integrative transpersonal 45–47; person-centred 40–43, 103–106, 129; pluralistic 45–47; psychodynamic 43–45
Murdin, Lesley 16, 40

Nicholson, Michelle 48–49, 121–122
non-verbal communication 20–23, 28–29, 41; uptalk 21–22, 29; vocal characteristics (pitch, tone intonation) 3–5, 20–21, 22, 23–24, 37, 48, 79, 96, 113, 132; vocal fry 22–23

old-age clients 106–107
online security 54, 132

paralanguage 20–23, 25, 26, 28–29, 41
Pearce, Peter 112
personality styles 28
person-centred therapy 40–43, 103–106, 129
phone therapy: accessibility 13–14, 45, 48, 57, 65, 91, 101, 106, 126; benefits/attributes and limitations 12–13, 16–17; define, setting 10–11; disinhibition effect (*see* disinhibition/disinhibition

effect); distractions, interruptions 18, 31, 69, 132; vs face-to-face counselling 1, 16, 17–19, 25, 41–49; vs helplines 11–12; intimacy 2, 6, 15, 18, 34, 41–42, 44, 47; modality adaptation 40–51; psychological suitability 76, 78–79, 134–135; risk management, client (*see* risk management, client); risk management, technology 53–57; supervision 126–137 (*see also* supervision by phone); therapeutic alliance, core skills 24–38
pitch, voice 4; *see also* vocal characteristics (pitch, tone intonation)
pluralistic therapy approach 48–49
Pollock, Karen 103–106
privacy 55, 67–69; data protection, GDPR 56, 61, 64–65; digital footprint 55; session settings, eavesdropping 7, 18, 49, 58, 60, 66, 97, 109–110, 132; settings (phone, internet, devices) 54, 55, 56–57; visual privacy 15, 35; *see also* confidentiality
psychodynamic psychotherapy 43–45
psychological suitability, phone therapy 76, 78–79, 134–135
psychological types 28

race and culture 98–102; acting out 102; addressing differences 100, 102; assumptions avoidance 99; confidentiality and trust 100–101; location of self, intersectional identities 99, 100; mirroring societal power dynamics, avoiding 99, 101, 102; naming/addressing differences 98; technology access 101; therapist/societal gaze 101–102
Reese, Robert J. 13–14
Reeves, Andrew 77–78
risk management, client 76–88; client–therapist confidentiality vs disclosure duties (*see* confidentiality); crisis situations 79–81; immediate risk management plan *82*, 111; legislation and statutory frameworks 81 (*see also* legal consideration); positive risk-taking 79–80; psychological suitability assessment 78–79; safeguarding referral, signposting 80, 86; suicidal ideation, self-harm 79–80; therapy framework 76–77
Rosenfield, Maxine 23, 31, 32, 40, 50, 66

Sanders, Pete 1, 26, 31, 32
Schneider, Paul L. 16, 26–27
security and confidentiality, technology
    53–56; digital footprint, therapist's 55;
    eavesdropping 55; hacking 55; online
    security 54, 132; recording sessions 56;
    voice activated devices 55–56
selective attention, theories 6
sessions: ending session 69–70; first
    session 65–66; privacy 67–69 (see also
    privacy); recording 56; technical issues,
    managing 56; transition time, managing
    18–19, 69–70; verbal contracting,
    boundary setting 66–67
Sewell, Ros 112
Sharpe, Tanja 115–120
silence 5, 16, 27, 30–31, 44, 93, 94, 102,
    106, 114
social model of disability 92, 93
sound, degraded 7–8
sound as emotion trigger 2, 4, 8
sound pathway 3–4
sound waves, frequency, amplitude,
    pitch 4
Stratton, Donna 43–45
substance abuse 49, 82–86, 85–86
sudden noise 4–5, 37
Suler, John 14, 33–35
supervision by phone 126–137; adapting
    face-to-face supervision 127–131;
    choosing a phone supervisor 136–137;
    discussing: communication skills
    development 132; discussing:
    equality, diversity and inclusion
    (EDI) 133–134; discussing: legal,
    professional and ethical issues 132;
    discussing: psychological suitability,
    risk management 134–135; online
    supervision 126–127; supervisee's
    context, legal implication 135–136;
    supervision agreement 131–132
Sweetman, Judith 95–98

technology 10–11, 53–57, 65, 97–98,
    127–128
tenuous contact 112, 113

'The Online Disinhibition Effect' (Suler)
    14, 33–35
therapeutic modalities; see modality
    adaptation for phone therapy
therapeutic phone alliance, core skills
    24–38; assumptions and bias, avoiding
    37–38; contact, making and maintaining
    26–27; disinhibition, managing 36–37;
    emotion, recognising and reacting to
    28–32; empathy, communicating 21, 25,
    41, 133; psychological processes, self-
    presentation 33–38; verbal nods 25–26,
    94, 106, 129; voice, effective use 23–24
tone, voice; see vocal characteristics
    (pitch, tone intonation)
toxic disinhibition 34–35, 105
trans clients; see gender, sexual and
    relationship diversity (GSRD)
transference, countertransference 44–45,
    46, 88, 129
Treisman, Anne 6

UK Council for Psychotherapy (UKCP)
    64, 70; Guidelines for working online
    or remotely (2021) 70, 90, 108, 110;
    safeguarding guidelines (2018) 81
uptalk 21–22, 29

validation, audible 25–26, 129
verbal nods 25–26, 94, 106, 129
virtual private network (VPN) 54
visual privacy 15, 35
visualisation 47, 85, 115, 121, 122–123;
    see also creative interventions
vocal characteristics (pitch, tone
    intonation) 3–5, 22, 23–24, 37, 48, 79,
    96, 113, 132
vocal fry 22–23, 29
voice, therapist's 23–24

Wanlass, Janine 130, 136
Wilson, Timothy D. 87
Willcox, Gloria 119

young people; see children and young
    people (CYP)

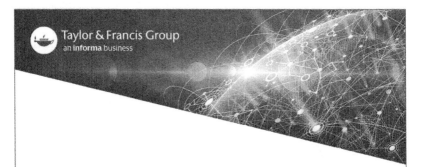